CARLA HALL'S
SOUL FOOD

ALSO BY CARLA HALL

Carla's Comfort Foods

Cooking with Love

CARLA HALL'S SOUL FOOD

Everyday AND *Celebration*

CARLA HALL

with Genevieve Ko

HARPER WAVE

HarperCollins books may be purchased for educational, business, or sales promotional use. For information, please e-mail the Special Markets Department at SPsales@harpercollins.com.

FIRST EDITION

Designed by Leah Carlson-Stanisic

Photography by Gabriele Stabile

Hall, Carla, and Ko, Genevieve.
Carla Hall's soul food : everyday and celebration / Carla Hall with Genevieve Ko.
p.   cm.
ISBN 978-0-06-266983-4
1. African American cooking. 2. Cooking, American—Southern style. I. Cookbooks.
TX715.2.A47 H34   2018
641.5975—dc23   2018020071

18 19 20 21 22   LSC   10 9 8 7 6 5 4 3 2 1

To all my ancestors, whom I call upon daily for strength and inspiration.

In memory of George Hall.

Contents

BEANS

121

CORNMEAL

141

BREADS

155

POULTRY

171

MEAT

195

CARLA HALL'S SOUL FOOD

Introduction

I've been eating soul food all my life and cooking it my whole career. I don't just know soul food. Soul food is *in* my soul. This book is a collection of my favorite recipes. It combines easy weeknight meals centered on seasonal vegetables with rich celebration dishes for special occasions. Even though the recipes have roots in history and heritage, they're my present-day twists on the classics and my original creations.

By definition, soul food refers to the dishes of the Cotton Belt of Georgia, Mississippi, and Alabama that traveled out to the rest of the country during the Great Migration. (The term itself came around the middle of the twentieth century.) You know what travels well? Fried chicken. Mac and cheese. Delicious, but not what anyone's meant to eat every day. I'm here to redefine soul food, to reclaim it.

Soul food is the true food of African-Americans.

The roots of our cooking are in West Africa. And from there, the American South, from the slave ports along the eastern coast to the southern border. We relied on seasonal vegetables, beans, and grains, with meat on rare occasions. Let's be clear: those were horrible times of suffering under the most unspeakable evil. I don't want to romanticize any of it. Not even the food. Remember, we didn't get to choose what we ate. But we made the most delicious dishes from what little we had. And what we cooked for the slave owners effectively became what we know as "American" food today.

After emancipation, African-Americans relied on the land and water for their daily meals. Collards in winter, peas through spring, tomatoes come summer. Chickens were for laying eggs, not frying. Fish and shrimp were abundant for coast and river folks. We lost that connection during the Great Migration and in the decades since as industrialized convenience food has made us unhealthy and sick. Our celebration foods—smoked whole hogs, candied yams, caramel cake—became what we ate all the time. We forgot about all the amazing daily meals we created from greens and beans and grains.

This book shines a light on those everyday foods my people were eating for generations in the South. That, my friends, is as much soul food as our celebration meals.

You may be wondering, "What's the difference between Southern food and soul food?" Easy answer: black cooks. And I'm one of them. A lot of the dishes, seasonings, and techniques are the same, but there's an extra *oomph* in soul food. It's like the difference between a hymn and a spiritual. Both sound beautiful and express the same message, but the spiritual's got a groove. Southern food's delicious any which way, but when it's made in the Black-American tradition with influences from Africa and the Caribbean, it delivers the kind of warmth and joy that makes you want to get up and dance.

I got that soul food in my bones. I was born into it in the South, with roots that go back generations. I grew up dunkin' cornbread into pot likker at the table, snapping green beans for church suppers, slicing chess pie at every baby shower and graduation party. At my very core, I'm always going back home to Tennessee when it comes to what I cook and eat. I've got a Nashville-born-and-bred palate, which marries heat and spice with tart and tangy and a sweetness that's not too sugary. Coming from that heritage, I got a hold on the food with the *soul* that bears its name.

For this book, I tried to imagine what my ancestors would be cooking from the farm if they were alive today. By looking to our roots, I'm showing you how delicious and healthy true soul food is. African-Americans were cooking farm-to-table centuries before it was a label to slap on hip restaurants. Foraging, pickling, preserving—that's how we survived. Our farms were all "organic." You think you discovered kale? Child, we've been eatin' those greens for hundreds of years. I'm going back to all that.

The bulk of this book is vegetable-centric weeknight recipes so comforting they taste like big ol' hugs. Just like the celebration foods. Even though I don't think you should eat feast foods every day, I still love 'em. You'll find my spins on the celebration foods that've been passed down by black cooks for generations for Sunday suppers, holidays, Juneteenth, family reunions, and parties.

Everything in this book will be fresher and lighter than most recipes out there. That's how I've always

cooked. I'm never consciously thinking about how to cut calories or fat or anything like that. What I am always doing is trying to make the main ingredients shine as much as possible—and that results in lighter dishes.

Granny, my greatest inspiration in the kitchen, raised me on good-for-you soul food. Granny was a dietician at a hospital and prepared meals at home for her husband, who needed heart-healthy dishes. She never skimped on flavor or made anything too lean, but cut back where she could. I'm pickin' up the torch and adding my own twists to Granny's dishes. The recipes in this book capture all the soulfulness of soul food but don't make you feel like you're gonna die afterward.

Or during the cooking process. I keep it all easy. Mama didn't teach me how to cook—because she didn't know how to cook well herself. Neither of my grandmothers taught me either, even though they both whipped up the best food I've had to this day. So if you're not experienced in the kitchen, I know where you're coming from 'cause I've been there. I want present and future generations to preserve true soul food, and I know the recipes need to be easy for that to happen. I've made the dishes in here super-simple after years of streamlining meals for busy home cooks as a host of *The Chew*. For all the everyday dishes, I keep the cooking times short and cut out extra pans and fuss wherever I can.

This book is about so much more than food. It collects and re-creates soul food memories. My personal ones, of course, but also communal ones among African-Americans. By drawing on memories in the kitchen, I re-create not only the taste of the dishes, but also the deep joy and comfort in sharing them. Now *that's* cooking with love. Anyone making this book's recipes will feel like they're at the family table and taste the deep roots of the food. This isn't just a collection of anonymous recipes, it's an intimate taste of true soul food.

Soul food needs to continue growing and evolving as a cuisine, and I hope this book is a part of it. Even though my Southern palate remains at the root of my cooking, my experiences with international cuisines and my farm-to-table instincts result in dishes that simultaneously have big, satisfying flavors but also feel bright and light.

Yes, this book celebrates soul food. And that means it celebrates American food. Because that's what soul food is—a cuisine created on this land. This book champions delicious dishes everyone will love and will show you how to embrace it as your own.

THE JOURNEY

Nashville was a great place to grow up. Maybe it'd be nice to retire there too. But I needed to be somewhere else in between. To get some perspective before I could come back. Mama's from a well-respected doctor's family and raised me and my sister, Kim, on the "good" side of town. Still, I got slurs thrown at me. Some boys even spat on me.

Despite that disgusting racism and prejudice, I was comfortable with my African-American identity *and* hanging out with white folks. My best friend Karen was white, and we had a grand ol' time playing together. Granny gathered my cousins, aunts, and uncles for Sunday supper each week after we spent the day at our historically black churches. My theater troupe was totally mixed, but we felt more connected to each other than to all the other kids.

Then I went to Howard for college. *Woke.*

Then Europe to model. In London, I cured homesickness with soul food.

Back in Washington, D.C., I started a lunch delivery service. My soups, sandwiches, and pound cakes fueled the guys at the barbershops. I found my life's passion in the kitchen, so I went to culinary school.

Like a lot of African-Americans who go to cooking school, I couldn't run fast enough from soul food as soon as I was taught European dishes. Early in my career, I was like, "Now I'm educated and I don't need to do soul food. You can't pigeonhole me in mac and cheese." Once I learned traditional French techniques, I got all uppity. I stopped frying chicken and started stewing it in red wine. With my European cooking, I rose through fancy restaurant ranks to become executive chef, private-cheffed for the super-rich, started my own catering company. Then I showed the world what I could do as a contestant on *Top Chef*.

In the intensity of the competition, I found my way home. When the pressure to win felt almost unbearable, I remembered what Granny always told me: "It's your job to be happy, not rich. If you do that, then everything else will follow." Nothing makes me happier than Granny's food. So I started cooking it, working in techniques I'd learned in professional kitchens. The judges, fellow contestants, viewers—everyone—could feel the love in my food.

Cooking soul food with love got me into the *Top Chef* finals and voted fan favorite. That opened the door for me to become one of the hosts on ABC's *The Chew*. Over my past six years of cooking for millions of Americans on TV, it's been all about coming back to soul food.

That was the inspiration for this book.

To really return to my roots, I knew I had to go back home. I had to travel the route so many African-Americans did before me, so I took a Southern road trip with my writer, Genevieve; and photographer, Gabriele. We started where the slave ships came into Charleston, South Carolina. From there, south along the sea islands of the Gullah-Geechee communities to

CARLA HALL'S SOUL FOOD

Savannah, Georgia. Inland to Civil Rights landmarks through-out Alabama. Up through the bittersweet beauty of the Mississippi Delta. Back home to Tennessee.

Along the way, we shared meals and stories with African-American farmers, chefs, cooks, legends. On farms, at markets, in restaurants, at home. Always breaking bread at the welcome table. And we traveled through time.

SELMA

I went to Selma for the first time on the road trip for this book. As soon as I started up the bridge, I felt it. The energy. Of the marchers. Of my ancestors. Sharecroppers. Slaves. My tears started and wouldn't stop. I didn't want them to. There's power in those honest emotions. The pull of the bridge was so strong, I had to touch it. I had to lie against the steel to feel it. All that energy.

The torture we endured. The death, the loss of dignity, all of it. We need to remember it and keep it in the forefront and acknowledge that it happened. What we have came at a serious cost. But when our bodies were broken, we held on to our souls.

With my back against the bridge, I felt the resistance and strength and unity. The fellowship of our people and how we share food. No matter how little you had, you always had enough to share.

And then I felt pride. Everyone I talked to on the trip—and all the African-Americans I've known who feed others—take pride in their food. We all should. There may have been times when, as black people, we didn't feel proud of that food history. At Selma, I went back in time and looked at this history and said I'm not ashamed of soul food. I'm proud of it. This is part of our heritage.

The sky went from gray to gold, the sun through the clouds. The light in the darkness. I was cleansed. I rose from the bridge's railings. Walked to the middle of it, where Dr. King and hundreds of others endured pain and hate to overcome. Their march was not in vain.

All of those emotions are in these recipes. They're soul food, coming from my soul. Yes, they're Southern too, but not in the way some understand Southern food. Those hot spots in the nicer neighborhoods where foodies are discovering "real" Southern food? Those places are built on the backs and shoulders of African-American cooks. You may not see many African-Americans as executive chefs of Michelin-starred restaurants, topping lists, or winning the big awards. Not yet. You don't see us, but we're here. We're in hotel kitchens, at catering companies, on the line at those starred places. We've always been here. And we're rising.

Now, I'm here to help y'all see us. Because, yes, you can see me. But I don't want you to ever think that I'm better than you are, better than any other chef out there. I certainly don't. But I've been blessed with this platform. I'm using it to say: I want all of us to be proud of soul food. Soul food is ours. Claim it. Reclaim it. I'm just here to share a taste.

Welcome to my table.

For this book, I tried to imagine what my ancestors would be cooking from the farm if they were alive today.

How to Cook from This Book

Any way you want! But here are a few pointers:

Everyday dishes work well on weeknights. Some are one-pot meals, but most—especially the vegetables—are meant to be on the table with other plates. Follow the Southern cafeteria-style dining concept of meat and three, where you choose a bit of meat and then three vegetable sides. Often, I just do the three. You can try that too.

Celebration dishes should be reserved for holidays, gatherings, and parties. Yes, because they're rich, but also because they're a commitment of time and energy. Cook them with friends and family members for a good time. To round out a party menu (see page 307), make lots of the everyday vegetables, which taste special enough for company.

Follow the formulas first, then play around. If you're already a pro in the kitchen, you can skim my recipes for inspiration and go at it. If you're just learning how to cook or don't feel too confident in the kitchen, measure the ingredients and follow the instructions carefully. The process will teach you how to balance flavor and texture.

Taste and season. I give measured salt amounts because folks often season too much or too little. Try my measured amounts, but always taste as you cook to see whether you need more or less salt. (If less, just hold off on adding any more while cooking.)

INGREDIENTS

Soul food's American food, so you'll find everything you need for these recipes in your local supermarket. I'm here to shine a light on ingredients that originated in Africa or are prevalent in the Caribbean. Those should be easy to find too—if not in a brick-and-mortar, then online. You'll find out more about the ingredients in their recipes.

- Since this book champions farmers, past and present, go find them! Buy their wares at their stands or in farmers' markets.

- Meat's something I enjoy in moderation. So when I get some, I go organic. It's pricey, but if it's a once-in-a-while meal, it's worth spending more to ensure the meat's good for you and the earth.

- Get Diamond Crystal Kosher Salt if you can. That's what I used for the measurements of savory dishes in this book. Morton's Kosher Salt is saltier and David's Kosher Salt saltier still. And don't swap in table salt for kosher. If you use anything but Diamond Crystal, start with less and taste before adding more. For baking, I use fine salt because it dissolves more readily. (I just call it "salt" in this book.)

- Vegetable oil in this book means any neutral-flavored oil, like canola, grape seed, or sunflower.

EQUIPMENT

You don't need anything fancy to cook these dishes, but a few things get used a lot:

- Sharp knives will change your life. Don't hack away with dull ones.

- Box grater and Microplane zester, for grating big and small.

- Cast-iron skillets are heavy and require care, but they're a cheap nonstick option that heats more evenly than anything else.

- Ditto Dutch ovens for soups, stews, and braises.

- Stand mixer if you want to bake a lot.

- Wooden spoons for mixing, silicone spatulas for scraping.

- Jars for keeping condiments.

Appetizers

Simple is good. Simple is easy to execute. Don't overthink things. Simple is often the best path to success.

Olive Oil Deviled Eggs

Celebration

6 large eggs, at room
temperature

1 tablespoon extra-virgin
olive oil

2 tablespoons mayonnaise

½ teaspoon Dijon mustard

¼ teaspoon kosher salt

Pinch of cayenne pepper

For a lighter, less cloying version of this soul food staple, I swap in some olive oil for some of the mayonnaise. It balances the creaminess of the filling and adds a fruity note.

Put the eggs in a medium saucepan and cover with cold water by 2 inches. Bring to a boil over medium-high heat, then add 1 cup ice. Reduce the heat and simmer for 10 minutes. Transfer to a bowl filled with ice and water. When cooled, peel and halve lengthwise.

Put the yolks in a bowl and add the oil, mayonnaise, mustard, salt, and cayenne. Mash and mix until smooth. Press the mixture through a fine-mesh sieve if you want an extra-silky filling. Transfer to a piping bag or resealable plastic bag with a hole snipped in one corner.

Pipe the filling into the egg white cavities and serve.

Make ahead: The deviled eggs can be refrigerated for up to 1 day.

Shortcut Deviled Eggs <u>WITH</u> Bread & Butter Pickles

MAKES 8	*Celebration*

4 large eggs

2 tablespoons mayonnaise

1 teaspoon Dijon mustard

Kosher salt and freshly ground black pepper

2 bread & butter pickle slices, diced

Snipped chives, for garnish

I often call soul food cooking with love. It may be because so many classics require so much TLC. Take deviled eggs. A party's not a party without them in the South. But you have to boil and peel those eggs, empty them, make a stuffing, and refill them. With this technique, I've streamlined the steps while keeping the soul of the dish intact. I soft-boil eggs, split them, then top them with a mayonnaise-mustard blend. The almost-set yolk is still creamy but stays in place. When you chew it, you end up with an even silkier version of all the yolky richness in a standard filling. No less love, but a lot less hassle.

Put the eggs in a small saucepan in a single layer and add enough cold water to cover by 1 inch. Bring to a boil over medium-high heat, then remove from the heat, cover, and let sit for 3 minutes. Transfer to a bowl of ice and water.

When the eggs are cool enough to handle, peel. Carefully cut each egg in half lengthwise (the yolks should be a little runny) and place on a serving plate, cut sides up.

Mix the mayonnaise and mustard with a pinch each of salt and pepper in a small bowl. Dollop the mixture over the yolks, then top with the pickles and chives. Serve immediately.

Deviled Egg Salad Sandwiches

MAKES 3 CUPS SALAD; ABOUT 3 DOZEN SANDWICHES

Celebration

6 large eggs

¼ cup mayonnaise

2 tablespoons sour cream

1 teaspoon Dijon mustard

¼ teaspoon kosher salt

⅛ teaspoon cayenne pepper

⅛ teaspoon freshly ground black pepper

2 teaspoons finely chopped fresh dill, plus sprigs for garnish

Angel Biscuits (page 162)

Cucumbers, cut in matchsticks, for garnish

Recipes are meant for sharing. When I taste something that blows my mind, I find out everything I can about it. That's what happened with this egg salad. I was at an event, took a bite of an egg salad sandwich, and screamed, "What the what?!" I felt like I was eating a deviled egg, but I was staring at egg salad! The chef who made it told me that the secret is tearing medium-cooked eggs by hand instead of cutting them with a knife. Those rustic irregular chunks end up feeling super-creamy in your mouth. I rushed home, tinkered with the seasonings, and hit on the blend here. To play up the deviled egg idea, I stuff the salad into biscuit rounds with cavities cut out of their tops the way you'd stuff an egg white with yolk filling. But this salad is just as delicious between slices of bread or by the spoonful.

Put the eggs in a medium saucepan and add enough cold water to cover them by 2 inches. Bring to a boil over medium-high heat, then cover, remove from the heat, and let stand for 7 minutes. Transfer the eggs to a bowl of ice and water.

Whisk the mayonnaise, sour cream, mustard, salt, cayenne, and black pepper in a large bowl. Peel the eggs, then tear them into ½-inch pieces with your fingers and drop them into the mayonnaise mixture. Add the dill and fold gently until everything is evenly coated.

Using a small serrated knife, cut a deep cavity in each biscuit by angling the knife toward the bottom of the biscuit while cutting off the top. Remove the tops and save to snack on later. Fill each biscuit cavity with the egg salad the way you would fill a deviled egg, mounding the salad above the top.

Garnish with cucumber and dill sprigs and serve immediately.

Black-Eyed Pea Hummus <u>WITH</u> Crudités

Everyday & *Celebration*

1 (15.5-ounce) can black-
    eyed peas, drained and
    rinsed

2 tablespoons tahini

1/4 teaspoon chile flakes

1 teaspoon apple cider
    vinegar

Kosher salt

1/2 cup extra-virgin olive oil

Crudités, for serving

Come to my table and I'll come to yours. Sharing food and recipes brings us together like nothing else. Sometimes I literally bring cultures together in my dishes. Here, I'm using a beloved African-American ingredient, the black-eyed peas that we eat for good luck on New Year's, in hummus, a Middle Eastern spread usually made with chickpeas. The black-eyed peas give this hearty dip a little personality and prove that mixing things up is a good thing.

Pulse the black-eyed peas in a food processor until finely ground. Add 3 tablespoons water and pulse until very smooth. If needed, add another tablespoon water to get the beans to a very smooth consistency.

Add the tahini, chile flakes, vinegar, and 1/2 teaspoon salt and process until incorporated. With the machine running, add the oil in a steady stream through the feed tube. Season to taste with salt.

Serve with crudités.

Make ahead: The hummus can be refrigerated for up to 1 week. Let it come to room temperature before serving.

Baked Blooming Onion
WITH Gruyère Cheese

2 jumbo onions

2 tablespoons extra-virgin olive oil

2 tablespoons dry white wine

1 teaspoon minced garlic

½ teaspoon minced fresh rosemary, plus leaves for garnish

Kosher salt and freshly ground black pepper

½ cup grated Gruyère cheese

1 small baguette, sliced and toasted

Here's my fresh spin on a familiar favorite. This is basically French onion soup as an appetizer spread. In culinary school, I learned how to caramelize onions and loved how they could melt in your mouth. You get the same effect without all the work when you let them collapse in the oven. The garlic, wine, and rosemary make them taste like the soup onions. So do the blanket of Gruyère on top and the baguette toasts you spread this hot mess on.

Preheat the oven to 375°F.

Trim the tops and bottoms of the onions, leaving the roots intact. Cut each onion from top to root into 12 wedges without cutting through the root. Put them side by side in an ovenproof baking dish that holds them snugly and fan out the onion petals.

Whisk the oil, wine, garlic, and rosemary in a small bowl. Pour over the open onion petals, then sprinkle with ½ teaspoon salt and ¼ teaspoon pepper. Cover the dish with foil.

Bake until the onions are tender, about 1½ hours. Uncover, sprinkle with the cheese, and return to the oven.

Bake until the cheese melts, about 10 minutes. Garnish with fresh rosemary leaves. Serve hot, scooping the cheesy onion onto baguette slices.

Grilled Celery WITH Pecans AND Cheddar Spread

2 ounces cream cheese, softened

1 tablespoon mayonnaise

1/4 small garlic clove, grated on a Microplane

1/16 teaspoon cayenne pepper

1 cup grated sharp yellow cheddar cheese

1 teaspoon vegetable oil

4 large celery stalks, tough strings removed with a vegetable peeler

1/4 cup pecans, toasted

Ants on a log were my favorite snack when I was a kid. This is my savory grown-up version. I pipe a spicy cheddar spread down celery, then press in toasted pecans. It's a great creamy-crunchy appetizer that feels indulgent but won't leave your guests too full for dinner. It's tasty with raw celery too.

Heat a grill or grill pan over high heat.

Mix the cream cheese, mayonnaise, garlic, and cayenne in a medium bowl until smooth. Fold in the cheddar cheese until evenly distributed. Transfer to a large resealable plastic freezer bag and massage to soften the cheese.

Rub the oil all over the celery stalks. Place on the hot grill grate or pan, curved side down, and grill until grill marks appear, about 8 minutes. Transfer to a cutting board. When cooled, cut into 4-inch lengths at an angle.

Snip a hole in the corner of the bag with the cheddar spread. Pipe the spread into the cavity of each celery stalk. Press the pecans into the spread. Serve immediately.

Make ahead: The cheddar spread can be refrigerated for up to 3 days. Soften before piping.

Harissa Spiced Nuts

¼ cup packed light brown sugar

1 tablespoon granulated sugar

1 tablespoon Harissa Spice Mix (page 242)

¾ teaspoon kosher salt

⅛ teaspoon coarsely ground black pepper

1 large egg white, at room temperature

2¼ cups mixed raw walnut halves, whole almonds, and pecan halves

Down South, we tell folks, "Do drop in!" And we mean it. When neighbors, friends, and family walk through the door unexpectedly, you'll want to have these nuts ready for them. Sweet, salty, and warm with spices, they're the nibble that'll make your guests feel like they can stay a while.

Preheat the oven to 300°F. Line a half-sheet pan with parchment paper.

Mix the brown sugar, granulated sugar, harissa, salt, and pepper in a small bowl. Whisk the egg white in a large bowl until stiff peaks form. Add the nuts and gently fold until the nuts are evenly moistened. Sprinkle the sugar and spice mixture on top and toss to coat evenly. Spread in a single layer on the prepared pan.

Bake, stirring and separating the nuts every 15 minutes, until golden brown, about 45 minutes.

Let cool on a wire rack, separating the nuts with two forks while they're still hot. Let cool completely.

Make ahead: The nuts keep at room temperature in an airtight container for up to 1 week.

Salt AND Pepper Butter Crackers

1½ tablespoons sugar

1 teaspoon table salt

⅔ cup cold water

1 cup all-purpose flour, plus more for rolling

1 cup whole wheat pastry flour

1 tablespoon baking powder

5 tablespoons cold unsalted butter, cut into ½-inch cubes, plus 2 tablespoons, melted

3 tablespoons vegetable oil

Kosher salt and freshly ground black pepper

Homemade crackers beat store-bought by a long shot. Especially these. They're flaky but sturdy, nutty from whole wheat, sweet from butter. Make them for parties, make them for snacks. Just make them. You can thank me later.

Whisk the sugar and table salt into the water in a small bowl until dissolved. In a food processor, pulse the all-purpose flour, whole wheat flour, and baking powder to mix. Add the cold butter cubes and oil and pulse until coarse crumbs form with a few pea-size pieces remaining. Add the water mixture all at once and pulse just until the dough comes together. Form into a 1-inch-thick rectangle, wrap tightly in plastic wrap, and refrigerate for 1 hour.

Preheat the oven to 400°F. Line 2 half-sheet pans with parchment paper.

On a lightly floured surface, using a lightly floured rolling pin, roll the dough into a rectangle ⅛ inch thick. Use a fluted 1½-inch square cookie cutter to cut out crackers. Place them on the prepared sheets, spacing them ½ inch apart.

Use a fork to poke 3 rows of holes in the center of each cracker. If the dough has softened too much, freeze until firm. Lightly brush the tops of the crackers with the melted butter. Sprinkle with kosher salt and pepper.

Bake, rotating the positions of the sheets halfway through, until golden brown, 15 to 20 minutes. Cool completely on the sheets on wire racks. The crackers will crisp as they cool.

Make ahead: The crackers keep at room temperature in an airtight container for up to 3 days.

Biscuit Crackers

MAKES AS MANY AS YOU WANT | *Everyday & Celebration*

Unsalted butter, for the pan

Flaky Buttermilk Biscuits (page 160)

Kosher salt

Cayenne pepper

Chances are you won't have any leftover biscuits. But if you do, you must make these crackers. As a matter of fact, they're worth making extra biscuits. They are so yummy! Crunchy, buttery, salty, spicy. Yassss-suh. You want these.

Preheat the oven to 350°F. Butter a half-sheet pan.

Cut the biscuits from top to bottom in ⅛-inch-thick slices. Place on the prepared pan, spacing ½ inch apart. Sprinkle with salt and cayenne.

Bake until the bottoms are golden brown, about 15 minutes. Flip and bake until the other sides are golden brown, about 10 minutes.

Let cool completely on the pan.

Make ahead: The crackers keep at room temperature in an airtight container for 1 day.

Pimento Cheese

Celebration

2 garlic cloves, grated on a Microplane

1 whole roasted red bell pepper, peeled, seeded, and chopped (½ cup)

4 ounces cream cheese, softened

½ cup mayonnaise

1 teaspoon cayenne pepper

½ teaspoon kosher salt

8 ounces sharp cheddar cheese, grated (2 cups)

8 ounces Monterey Jack cheese, grated (2 cups)

This is *the* party cheese y'all. You've gotta have some if you're throwing one. And if you do have some, anyone who comes over will think you're having a party. There's nothing easier than pimento cheese, but I like to make mine in a mixer. It smashes the cheese into the creamy base, softening it into the spread while leaving something to chew on. Serve this with crackers (pages 27–28) as an appetizer or slather on bread to make a sandwich.

Combine the garlic, bell pepper, cream cheese, mayonnaise, cayenne, and salt in the bowl of a stand mixer with the paddle attachment. Beat on medium-low speed until well mixed, scraping the bowl occasionally. Add the cheddar and Monterey Jack cheeses and beat on low speed until the cheese is evenly distributed.

Transfer to a serving bowl, cover with plastic wrap, and refrigerate for at least 1 hour and preferably overnight. The garlic will mellow over time and the flavors will meld.

Make ahead: The cheese can be refrigerated for up to 1 week.

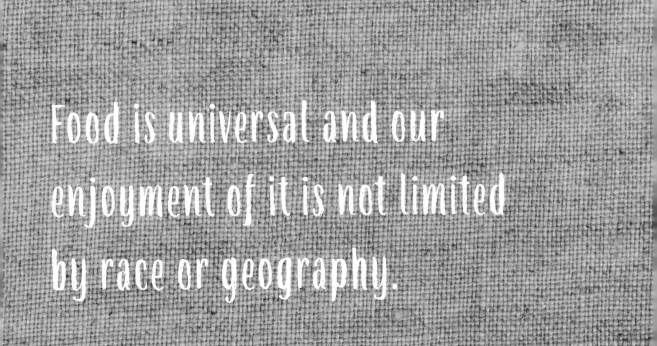

Food is universal and our enjoyment of it is not limited by race or geography.

Vegetables

Mixed Bitter Greens <u>WITH</u> Smoked Trout Pot Likker

SERVES 8

Everyday & Celebration

3 tablespoons extra-virgin olive oil

2 onions, cut into very thin half-moons

Kosher salt

2 garlic cloves, grated on a Microplane

1/4 teaspoon chile flakes

1 tablespoon apple cider vinegar

2 fillets smoked trout

1 pound leafy sturdy bitter greens, such as collards or kale, tough stems removed, leaves cut into 1/2-inch ribbons crosswise

1 pound leafy tender bitter greens, such as dandelion or chard, tough stems removed, leaves cut into 1/2-inch ribbons crosswise

For centuries, a mess of greens graced the tables of African-Americans. But they weren't just collards. Anything dark and leafy and coming up out of the earth found its way into the stew pot: turnip, dandelion, mustard, kale, and beet greens, to name just a few. All have a pleasant bitter edge that mellows when the greens are slow-simmered with vinegar and smoky meat. Choose whichever greens look the perkiest, with no blemishes or rotted spots.

Pork jowls and ham hocks are commonly cooked with greens, but I use smoked trout for a lighter take. You can find it in the refrigerated seafood section of your market. It makes for a super-flavorful pot likker, which is all that seasoned juice left from cooking the greens. It's been a staple of African-American diets since the beginning. In documented interviews from the 1930s, ex-slaves spoke of "potlicker." What others may have wasted, we saved. That savory broth tastes delicious swirled back into the greens, soaked into cornbread, and as stock for other dishes.

Heat the oil in a large Dutch oven over medium heat. Add the onions and 1 teaspoon salt. Cook, stirring occasionally, for 2 minutes. Add the garlic and cook, stirring, for 1 minute. Stir in the chile flakes and vinegar and simmer for 3 minutes. Add 2 cups water and bring to a boil. Fold in 1 trout fillet and the sturdy greens until well mixed. Cover, reduce the heat to low, and simmer until the greens are very tender, about 45 minutes.

Discard the trout. Return the mixture to a boil over medium heat. Fold in the tender greens, cover, reduce the heat to medium-low, and simmer until tender, about 5 minutes. Stir in 1/2 teaspoon salt. Taste and add more salt if you'd like.

Remove the greens from the heat. Peel off and discard the skin of the remaining trout fillet and flake the meat. Transfer the greens with their pot likker to a serving dish and top with the trout.

Creamed Kale

2 cups heavy cream

4 garlic cloves, very thinly sliced

½ teaspoon chile flakes

½ teaspoon freshly grated nutmeg

1 onion, finely chopped

Kosher salt and freshly ground black pepper

2 tablespoons vegetable oil

3 bunches Tuscan kale (about 2 pounds total), tough stems removed, leaves cut into ¼-inch slices

I love creamed spinach, so I figured I'd really love creamed kale. I was right! Because the leaves are so much sturdier, they don't break down in the sauce or release much water. That means a more satisfying chew with each bite and more nutrients too. This may sound like a trendy take on a classic, but kale's been a soul food staple for hundreds of years. Everyone's figuring out now what we've known forever: kale really is delicious.

Bring the cream to a boil in a large pot over medium-high heat. Boil until reduced to 1½ cups. Add the garlic, chile flakes, nutmeg, half the onion, 1 teaspoon salt, and ¼ teaspoon pepper. Bring to a boil, then reduce the heat to medium and simmer, stirring occasionally, for 15 minutes.

Meanwhile, heat the oil in a large skillet over medium-high heat. Add the remaining onion and ½ teaspoon salt. Cook, stirring often, for 1 minute. Reduce the heat to medium and add the greens, a handful at a time, stirring to wilt after each addition. Stir in ½ teaspoon salt. Cover and cook, stirring occasionally, until tender, about 10 minutes.

Uncover and grab a bunch of the greens with tongs to squeeze out any excess water. Transfer to the cream mixture. Repeat with the remaining greens. Stir well to coat with the cream mixture. Serve hot.

On September 11, 2001, Cindy Ayers Elliott knew it was time to leave Manhattan and return home to Jackson, Mississippi. After the terror attacks, she was convinced of how much more she wanted to do with her life than investment banking. She traded her high heels for work boots and founded Foot Print Farms, where she and her fellow farmers grow fruits and vegetables and raise livestock. They welcome the community to farm on the land, harvest the crops, and taste their wares at local farm markets. Cindy says, "I know for sure this is where I'm supposed to be at this time. I'm not making nearly as much money as I used to make, but I have more than I've ever had."

Part of Cindy's mission is to teach kids—and adults— how to eat all of these fruits and vegetables. When she first started sharing her produce with the local community, she got a lot of blank stares if she handed out bunches of greens and herbs. She realized that her neighbors were so far from their great-grandmothers' cooking that they didn't even know where to start. Cindy and her team began teaching them old-school soul food staples like fresh mint tea and callaloo. Now, the community members swap recipes and ideas on their own, often with the kids leading the conversation. Cindy took her Jackson community back to its roots to move it forward, with lots of beautiful vegetables along the way.

Caramelized Leek AND Mustard Green Soup WITH Chow Chow

SERVES 6	Everyday

2 tablespoons extra-virgin olive oil

1 tablespoon unsalted butter

2 leeks, white and pale green parts only, cut into thin half-moons (4 cups)

Kosher salt

4 large garlic cloves, smashed and peeled

1 teaspoon chile flakes

1/2 cup Harvest Chow Chow (page 254) or store-bought chow chow, plus more for serving

4 cups low-sodium vegetable broth

8 cups packed chopped mustard greens or kale

When cooking for themselves, slaves had to stretch what little they had. The spirit of making the most out of humble ingredients lives on here, where I turn one bunch of fresh greens into a big ol' pot of soup. To give the broth a one-two punch of tangy yum, I blend chow chow, a classic Southern pickle relish, right into the mix, then dollop more on top right before serving. With each steamin' spoonful, I go from *ooh!* with the bright pickles and bite of the spicy greens to *ahh* with the creamy sweetness of caramelized leeks.

Heat the oil and butter in a large Dutch oven over medium heat until the butter melts. Add the leeks and 1/2 teaspoon salt. Cook, stirring occasionally, until almost tender, about 5 minutes. Add the garlic and 1/2 teaspoon salt and cook, stirring often, until the leeks are tender, about 4 minutes. Stir in the chile flakes.

Meanwhile, puree the 1/2 cup chow chow with 1 cup broth in a blender until smooth. Add to the leeks along with the remaining 3 cups broth, 2 cups water, and 1/2 teaspoon salt. Bring to a boil, then reduce the heat and simmer for 20 minutes.

Add the greens and stir gently just until wilted, 1 to 2 minutes. Remove from the heat and transfer to the blender. Pulse until the greens are finely chopped. Taste and add more salt if you'd like. Divide among serving bowls and top with more chow chow.

Coconut Callaloo Soup

SERVES 6	*Everyday*

2 tablespoons coconut oil

1 large green bell pepper, seeded and chopped

1 small onion, chopped

4 garlic cloves, smashed

Kosher salt and freshly ground black pepper

2 sprigs fresh thyme

1 habanero chile, slit

1 cup sliced fresh okra

3 cups unsalted vegetable broth

1 (15-ounce) can coconut milk

1 russet potato, peeled and chopped

1 bay leaf

1 large bunch spinach, chopped (5 cups)

Callaloo describes both the leafy greens from taro, dasheen, tania, amaranth, and yautia plants and the name of the dish made from those greens. Whether the dish originated in West Africa, Trinidad, Tobago, or Jamaica remains contested. Its deliciousness is not. The greens simmer to silkiness in either palm or coconut oil, often with chiles and crab. I turned it into a vegetable-only soup, doubling up on coconut with oil and milk. If you can find callaloo greens, use them. Otherwise, buy a big bunch of spinach. Yes, the boxed baby stuff is convenient, but fresh bunches from the ground have much more flavor. Trim the ends, but keep the stems and chop them too. They'll all soften together in this creamy soup.

Heat the oil in a large Dutch oven over medium heat. Add the bell pepper, onion, garlic, and 1 teaspoon salt. Cook, stirring occasionally, until the onion is just translucent, about 3 minutes. Add the thyme and chile and cook, stirring often, for 3 minutes. Add the okra and cook, stirring often, until tender, about 5 minutes.

Add the broth, coconut milk, potato, bay leaf, and 1 teaspoon salt. Bring to a boil over high heat, then reduce the heat to low. Simmer until the potato is very tender, about 30 minutes.

Discard the bay leaf, thyme, and chile. Transfer half of the mixture to a blender and puree until smooth. Return to the heat and stir in the spinach. Season with salt and pepper. Serve hot.

Chopped Salad with Buttermilk Dressing

½ cup buttermilk

½ cup mayonnaise

2 tablespoons fresh or bottled horseradish

½ small garlic clove, grated on a Microplane

2 tablespoons apple cider vinegar

¼ teaspoon cayenne pepper

Kosher salt and freshly ground black pepper

15 cups chopped vegetables, for the salad

The dressing makes the salad here. It's tangy, creamy, and just the right kind of hot. The sharp bite of horseradish intensifies with a little cayenne and black pepper, then mellows in buttermilk and mayo. In the summer, toss this with tomatoes, cucumber, and corn. In winter, it's nice over shredded kale or brussels sprouts. Spring and all year round, it's yummy with chopped salad greens, carrots, and radishes. You can toss in herbs like dill and parsley or crunchies like toasted pecans or cornbread croutons. This is your salad, baby. Make it your way.

Whisk the buttermilk, mayonnaise, horseradish, garlic, vinegar, cayenne, ½ teaspoon salt, and ½ teaspoon black pepper in a medium bowl until smooth. You should have 1¼ cups dressing.

Toss the chopped vegetables in a large bowl. Season lightly with salt and toss again. Drizzle on just enough dressing to coat and toss gently until everything's skimmed with dressing. Serve the salad with more dressing on the side for anyone who wants it.

Make ahead: The dressing can be refrigerated for up to 3 days.

Jones Valley Teaching Farm covers a big city block in downtown Birmingham. Across the street from project housing, catty-corner from the schoolyard's playing fields, within sight of a big highway overpass. And near where chef John Hall grew up. He walked me up and down the garden rows one summer afternoon, plucking purple okra and popping the seeds like it ain't no thing. He told me what it's like to return home after cooking in Michelin-starred restaurants in Luxembourg and New York City.

"I didn't think in a million years I'd come back. But I feel an obligation to the community. To lead by example, teach up, coach up. Farm-to-table's how we always knew food to be in my family, with my grandfather's farm out in Alabama country. But I want to teach the kids here now how to cook and eat these vegetables."

John's feeding the city well through his restaurants and through this community farm program. And he taught me a thing or two. Hearing him crunch on raw okra reminded me that we can get the next generation to love vegetables if we cook them right. I flash back to my childhood: Screaming *eeew!* at the way slime dripped out of okra like a runny nose. Swearing I'd never eat that nasty thing. But I'm grown now. I know that okra turns slimy only when stewed too long, so let's all unite in barely cooking it at all. For the sake of the children.

As mosquitoes chased us out of the green bean vines at dusk, John said, "What I love about this place is that it gets vegetables in the kids' minds early. They attach the good food here to a good way of life." Amen to that.

Seared Okra

1 pound okra, halved
    lengthwise

1 tablespoon extra-virgin
    olive oil

1/2 teaspoon kosher salt

This is for all the people who hate okra because it's slimy. Liking okra's in my DNA. It's native to Africa and it's a major Southern crop. Even so, I used to hate it. It's a texture thing. But *this*. This is a revelation. There's something about searing okra in a pan over really high heat that brings out its beauty. Crisp, charred, delicious. It's such a simple thing. You need a good ol' pot for this. The heavy cast-iron kind that used to hang over an open fire. You also better have your plate ready to go. When you know you need to get these out of the pan, you've got to be ready.

Get a big cast-iron pan smoking hot over high heat.

Toss the okra, oil, and salt in a large bowl with your hands until the okra is evenly coated. Add the pieces to the hot pan cut side down, leaving space between them. Don't crowd the pan. You can sear them in batches.

Sear until nearly blackened, about 2 minutes per side. Transfer to a plate and serve hot, warm, or at room temperature.

Grilled Okra ⎯WITH⎯ Spiced Sprinkle

Okra, stems trimmed

Vegetable oil, for coating

Kosher salt

Barbecue Spice Blend
  (page 240), for
  sprinkling

When okra's fresh and plump in the summer, it's best barely cooked. With this quick grilling technique, it ends up as crunchy as a cucumber and smoky like barbecue. I sprinkle on the spice right after cooking so the residual heat from the grill takes the edge off the spices without burning them.

Prepare a charcoal grill for direct grilling over hot coals, or heat a gas grill or grill pan to high.

Toss the okra pods with just enough oil to slick them. Grill them, turning occasionally, until grill marks appear and the okra turns a shade darker, about 5 minutes. Immediately sprinkle with salt and the spice blend to coat. Serve hot, warm, or at room temperature.

Chunky Tomato Soup WITH Roasted Okra Rounds

SERVES 4	Everyday

1 pound okra, cut crosswise into ½-inch slices

2 tablespoons plus 4 teaspoons extra-virgin olive oil

Kosher salt and freshly ground black pepper

2 onions, diced

3 garlic cloves, sliced

2 carrots, diced

1 celery stalk, diced

½ teaspoon chile flakes

1 (14.5-ounce) can fire-roasted diced tomatoes

This. *This* is what this whole book is about. Revolutionizing soul food is about cooking faster and cleaner today. The old-school method for this soup required stewing until the broth got thick and gelatinous from the okra. Here, I keep the tomato broth superlight. I add cold water to quickly extract the flavors from the vegetables and I keep the okra out of it. Until the end, that is. I flash-roast okra rounds until they're as crunchy as fries. Those get scattered on just before chow time so they stay crisp. I start with indigenous ingredients—the tomato, onion, and garlic base of African stews and the okra prevalent in the South—and end with a fresh bowl of comfort.

Preheat the oven to 400°F with a half-sheet pan on the center rack.

Toss the okra, 4 teaspoons oil, and ½ teaspoon salt in a large bowl until the okra is evenly coated. Spread on the hot pan in a single layer. The okra should sizzle as soon as it hits the pan.

Roast until the okra is browned and crisp-tender, 20 to 25 minutes.

Meanwhile, heat the remaining 2 tablespoons oil in a Dutch oven over medium heat. Add the onions and ½ teaspoon salt. Cook, stirring, for 1 minute, then add the garlic. Cook, stirring occasionally, until tender, about 5 minutes. Add the carrots, celery, chile flakes, and ½ teaspoon salt. Cook, stirring often, for 2 minutes.

Add the tomatoes, 3 cans (from the empty tomato can) of cold water, and ½ teaspoon salt. Bring to a boil, then reduce the heat and simmer for 10 minutes. Season to taste with salt and pepper.

Divide the soup among individual bowls and top with the roasted okra. Serve immediately.

Cast-Iron Blackened Beans
WITH Lemon AND Chile

SERVES 8	Everyday

1¾ pounds flat (Romano) beans, tipped and tailed

3 tablespoons extra-virgin olive oil

½ teaspoon kosher salt

¼ teaspoon chile flakes

Lemon wedges, for serving

The tasty thread that runs through soul food is the trinity of sweet, heat, and sour. You can get a taste of it in ten minutes with this dish. The base is flat beans as wide as your thumb. My aunt grew these tough-skinned string beans in her garden and I loved when she slow-cooked them to silky softness. After moving north, I didn't see the beans anywhere. It wasn't until a recent trip to London that I had them again! Our hostess was a real hoot, but also a really great cook, and she dunked the flat beans from her garden into boiling water for less than a minute so they were still nice and chewy. She told me flat beans are sometimes labeled Romano beans. Once I made that connection, I realized that they were at my local markets!

To retain their grassy flavor and simultaneously get rid of their toughness, I sear these beans—hard—in a cast-iron skillet, then quick-steam them in the same pan. As they blister in the smokin' hot pan, they take on a lip-smacking char.

Tip: Look for perky beans with a smooth skin. If they're wrinkled or floppy, they'll taste tough after cooking.

Heat a large cast-iron skillet over high heat until smoking. Meanwhile, toss the beans, oil, and salt in a large bowl. Add the beans to the skillet and sear, turning occasionally, until browned in spots and soft enough to bend easily, about 6 minutes.

Add ¼ cup water, cover, and cook until the water evaporates, about 3 minutes. Uncover and toss in the chile flakes. Transfer to a serving dish and squeeze lemon juice on top. Serve hot.

Green Bean Salad ⎯WITH⎯ Pickled Red Onions

Everyday & Celebration

Kosher salt and freshly
   ground black pepper

1½ pounds green beans,
   tipped and tailed

1 teaspoon extra-virgin
   olive oil

Red Onion Pickles
   (page 255)

1 hot chile, very thinly
   sliced

In Granny's garden in Nashville, pole bean plants poked their little heads out in spring and ended up taller than me by summer. When I was little, Granny'd ask me to pluck the beans and I'd whine the whole way across the yard. But once I faced those vines, I'd be awed by the magic of their stalks. The pretty little tendrils looked thin as thread, but they had a monster grip on those garden stakes. And the beans, soft and dry as worn leather, nearly dripped juice when I snapped them. Every time I stopped to snack on my little harvest, I'd be shocked by how something so green could be so sweet. I try to capture that sweetness here by tossing blanched beans in a wisp of oil, salt, and pickle juice. In season, there's no need to smother fresh beans with tons of gravy! Simply cooked until bright and crisp, slender beans need only the pop of quick pickles.

Bring a large saucepan of water to a boil and generously salt it. Fill a large bowl with ice and cold water. Add the beans to the boiling water and boil until crisp-tender, about 5 minutes. Using tongs, transfer to the ice water. When cooled, drain well and transfer to a large bowl.

Toss the beans with the oil and 2 teaspoons liquid from the pickles. Season with salt and pepper. Top with the red onion pickles and chile and serve.

Make ahead: The cooked green beans can be refrigerated for up to 3 days.

Tomato, Cucumber, AND Dill Salad

SERVES 4	*Everyday & Celebration*

¼ cup distilled white or apple cider vinegar

⅓ cup extra-virgin olive oil

1 teaspoon sugar

¼ teaspoon chile flakes

Kosher salt and freshly ground black pepper

4 ripe tomatoes, cored, seeded, and cut into wedges

1 white onion, thinly sliced

1 seedless cucumber, sliced into half-moons

¼ cup celery leaves or parsley leaves, torn

2 tablespoons picked fresh dill

Summertime, and the livin' is easy. That's the feeling this salad delivers. Granny and Mama set it down all season long. Fat tomatoes, slick cucumbers, crisp onion dragged through dressing. That dill—like lying on cool grass. Altogether, a plate of goodness.

Whisk the vinegar, oil, sugar, chile flakes, 1 teaspoon salt, and ½ teaspoon pepper in a large bowl. Add the tomatoes, onion, cucumber, celery leaves, and dill. Toss to combine. Serve immediately.

Peach AND Tomato Salad

SERVES 6 | *Everyday & Celebration*

3 ripe peaches, pitted and cut into wedges

3 heirloom tomatoes, cored and cut into wedges

Kosher salt

2 teaspoons apple cider vinegar

1 tablespoon extra-virgin olive oil

1 tablespoon chopped fresh flat-leaf parsley

1 small red onion, halved and very thinly sliced

1 Cubanelle pepper, seeded and very thinly sliced

1/4 fresh hot chile, thinly sliced

Fresh herbs, such as parsley, chervil, tarragon, and dill, for serving

Maldon sea salt, for sprinkling

On the first night of our Southern road trip for this book, chef Marvin Woods invited us to his Charleston restaurant. After a night of dinner and dancing, he sent us on our way with armloads of summer tomatoes and peaches. We took those goods across four state lines before I had the time to turn them into the dish I'd been dreaming of. I wanted a refreshing savory salad, with crisp onion and pepper to offset the soft fruit. I craved a drizzle of vinaigrette and a shower of herbs. It was so simple to throw together and even easier to down. Spanish Arbequina olive oil has a fruity taste that pairs well with the tomatoes and peaches, so try to use it if you can.

Toss the peaches and tomatoes with 1/4 teaspoon kosher salt in a large bowl and let sit until juicy, about 5 minutes.

Meanwhile, whisk the vinegar, oil, and 1/4 teaspoon kosher salt in a small bowl. Add the parsley, onion, pepper, and chile to the peach mixture and toss to mix, then drizzle with the dressing and toss until evenly coated.

Spread on a serving platter and scatter the herbs and Maldon salt on top.

CARLA HALL'S SOUL FOOD

Tomato Pie with Garlic Bread Crust

SERVES 6	*Everyday* & *Celebration*

3 tablespoons extra-virgin olive oil, plus more for brushing

½ loaf country bread

5 ripe medium tomatoes

3 garlic cloves, grated on a Microplane

2 teaspoons fresh thyme leaves

Kosher salt

Tomato pie's a Southern staple. Often, the fruit's suspended in a creamy mayonnaise-and-cheese filling that's baked into a flaky crust. But the variations are endless, so here's mine. To get a lighter pie without struggling to keep the crust from sogging, I created a crust of garlic bread. It soaks up all those tomato juices while toasting to a crisp. With this six-ingredient bake, the tomatoes really get to shine.

Preheat the oven to 450°F. Brush a 9-inch square metal cake pan with oil.

Cut four 1-inch-thick slices from the loaf. Arrange them in a single layer in the bottom of the pan. They should cover the bottom. If they don't, cut more slices to fit. Brush the bread all over with oil. Bake until the bread is golden brown and well toasted, about 5 minutes.

Meanwhile, core the tomatoes. Trim the very tops and bottoms, then peel the tomatoes. Cut each in half through its equator. Mix the garlic and oil in a large bowl.

Arrange the tomatoes in a single layer over the bread. Gently smash them into the bread, then brush with the garlic oil. Sprinkle with 1 teaspoon thyme leaves and ½ teaspoon salt. Tear the remaining bread into 1-inch chunks and toss in the garlic oil until evenly coated. Scatter the torn bread and remaining 1 teaspoon thyme leaves over the tomatoes.

Bake until the top is golden brown and crisp and the tomatoes are juicy, about 30 minutes. Let cool slightly, then cut into squares and serve.

Panfried Corn with Tomatoes

SERVES 6	Everyday

6 ears corn, shucked and silked

2 very ripe tomatoes

2 tablespoons vegetable oil

1 onion, finely diced

Kosher salt

2 garlic cloves, very thinly sliced

1 tablespoon unsalted butter

¼ teaspoon cayenne pepper

Nowadays, Southern fried corn's loaded with butter, sugar, and bacon. I'm taking this dish back to its roots, making the corn sweet and creamy with its own starchy, sugary juices. Instead of overpowering the dish with bacon, I'm tossing in tomatoes and letting their tangy pulp melt into the mix. A touch of butter at the end binds it all together into a spoonable side dish.

If you have a gas stovetop, turn a burner to high. If not, heat a grill or grill pan to high. Put the corn over the fire to char, turning occasionally, until blackened in spots. When the corn is cool enough to handle, cut off the kernels and reserve. Hold a cob over a large dish and use the dull edge of the knife blade to scrape off any remaining pulp and the corn's juices. Repeat with the remaining cobs. Reserve the juices and pulp; discard the cobs.

Cut the tomatoes in half through their equators. If they're so ripe that they're wobbly, squeeze them by hand over a bowl to release all the juices, seeds, and fruity pulp. If they're too stiff to squeeze, grate the cut sides against the large holes of a box grater set over a bowl. Reserve the juicy stuff; discard the skins.

Heat the oil in a large skillet over medium heat. Add the onion and ½ teaspoon salt. Cook, stirring occasionally, until almost translucent, about 3 minutes. Add the garlic and cook, stirring, for 1 minute. Add the corn pulp and juices and ½ teaspoon salt. Cook, stirring, until thickened and starting to stick to the skillet, about 1 minute.

Add the tomato pulp and juices and ½ cup water. Cook, stirring and scraping up bits from the skillet. Once the liquid is simmering, add the butter and cayenne. Stir until the butter melts. Add the reserved corn kernels and stir until heated through. Serve hot.

Tomato, Basil, AND Mayonnaise Sandwiches

This is all I want all summer: juicy, ripe tomato slabs and fresh basil squishing into mayonnaise on good bread. It was my favorite sandwich when I was growing up. (Still is!) Weirdly, my sister, Kim, never tasted one until she stopped by the photo shoot for this book. What?! When I saw her eyes widen with her first bite, I got so excited. It reminded me of how giddy I felt the first time I ate one. Kim went on and on—"Oh, this is so good!"—and wanted to know how to make it. There's nothing to it, but here's how to put together a really great one:

- Good bread: The best base for this sandwich is freshly griddled Johnnycakes (page 142). The natural sweetness of the cornmeal makes tomatoes even tastier. When I don't have those ready to go—honestly, that's most of the time—I like cutting thick-ish slices from a country loaf with a crackly crust and a fine and sturdy yet soft inside. Too many holes and you'll have dripping issues. Too thin and tender will leave you with a soggy mess on your hands.

   Lay down those slices on a cutting board, matching the neighbors to come back together later.
- Lots of mayo: Go out and get Duke's Mayonnaise. If you live in the South, just pick some up at the store. Otherwise, order it online. Trust me. Its balance of creaminess and tang? Woo, child! Worth it.

   Now, take that superior spread and slather on enough to leave you wiping some from the corners of your mouth with each bite. Spread it just short of cake frosting style.
- Just right ripe tomatoes: Not too hard, but not too soft. You want something to chew in there without a dribbly mess on your shirt. Give the tomato a little squeeze. You're looking for the plump feel of a perfect peach. Feels like a wobbly water balloon? Save it for sauce.

   Cut those good tomatoes into 1/2-inch-thick slices through their equators. Snack on the ends and press the slices into the mayo on each sandwich bottom. Sprinkle them with coarse or flaky salt and grind on a little black pepper.
- Bits of basil: A little fresh bite is all you need to spark up your sandwich. Look for tender leaves that you can smell without sticking your nose into the bunch. Tear big leaves into bits or keep little ones whole. Scatter them all over those tomatoes.
- Turn the lonely slice of mayo-coated bread onto the tomato stack. Press to get the tomato juices oozing a little.
- Open your mouth wide. Wider. Take a big ol' bite. Repeat.

Succotash Salad ⎯WITH⎯ Corn ⎯AND⎯ Lima Beans

SERVES 6	*Everyday* & *Celebration*

3 tablespoons fresh lemon juice

1 garlic clove, smashed and minced

1 teaspoon sugar

1 teaspoon Dijon mustard

1 tablespoon plus 2 teaspoons apple cider vinegar

Kosher salt and freshly ground black pepper

3/4 cup frozen lima beans, thawed

1 tablespoon unsalted butter

1/2 sweet onion, chopped

1/4 cup vegetable oil

5 cups fresh corn kernels

2 cups cherry or grape tomatoes, halved

2 tablespoons sliced fresh basil leaves

Native American and African-American ties go way back. In cooking, the complex connections came through farming. We all understood that what grows together goes together. Native Americans planted together corn, beans, and squash, known as the three sisters. In the seventeenth century, the Narragansett Indians introduced starving colonists to "msickquatash," a stew of corn and beans. That name of the dish became Anglicized to "succotash" and it has spread across the country and evolved over the years to mean any dish with corn and beans.

In my interpretation, I'm going with summer succotash. And adding two of my favorite garden partners—tomatoes and basil. All tossed up with sunny fresh kernels and limas, they turn into a refreshing salad.

Whisk the lemon juice, garlic, sugar, mustard, 1 tablespoon of the vinegar, and 1/2 teaspoon salt in a large bowl. Let sit so the garlic mellows out.

Meanwhile, bring a small saucepan of salted water to a boil. Add the lima beans and boil until bright green and almost tender, about 2 minutes. Drain well, rinse under cold water until cool, and drain again.

Melt the butter in a large skillet over medium heat. Add the onion and 1/2 teaspoon salt. Cook, stirring occasionally, until the onion is translucent and tender but not browned, 5 to 7 minutes. Reduce the heat to medium-low; add the lima beans and 1/2 teaspoon salt; and cook, stirring, until the beans are crisp-tender, about 1 minute. Add 1/2 teaspoon salt and the remaining 2 teaspoons vinegar. Cook, stirring, until the liquid evaporates.

Whisk the lemon juice mixture again. While whisking, add the oil in a slow, steady stream and whisk until emulsified. Add the onion-bean mixture and the corn, tomatoes, and 1/2 teaspoon salt. Toss until well mixed.

When cooled and ready to serve, toss again and top with the basil and a generous grinding of black pepper.

Dilled Cucumber AND Celery Salad

Everyday & Celebration

¼ cup distilled white
   vinegar

1 teaspoon sugar

1 teaspoon kosher salt

2 cucumbers, peeled
   in strips, quartered,
   seeded, and thinly sliced

1 cup celery leaves or very
   thinly sliced celery

2 tablespoons picked fresh
   dill

Throw this bright little thing on any meaty dish to cut through the richness. It's great on Oxtail Stew (page 216) and Meatloaf (page 214).

Whisk the vinegar, sugar, and salt in a large bowl until the sugar dissolves. Add the cucumbers and toss to coat. Just before serving, toss in the celery leaves and dill.

Pickled Cucumber Salad

Everyday & Celebration

2 large cucumbers, peeled and sliced

Kosher salt and freshly ground black pepper

2 tablespoons apple cider vinegar

1/4 teaspoon sugar

1/4 teaspoon chile flakes

Dill sprigs, for garnish

On our road trip for this book, chef Joe Randall took us to Mrs. Wilkes Dining Room, a Savannah institution. You're seated and served family-style, with a spread of at least twenty classic Southern dishes. The one I kept returning to looked the humblest. It was a little bowl of cucumber slices. But each slice packed a pickle-y refreshing crunch from the two-step technique of salting the cucumber before marinating it. I re-created it here and added chile and dill. This is exactly what you need in a parade of rich dishes.

Arrange the cucumber slices on a large platter in a single layer. Sprinkle with salt and pepper, cover with plastic wrap, and refrigerate for 1 hour.

Whisk the vinegar, sugar, and chile flakes in a large bowl. Discard any accumulated juices on the cucumber platter. Add the cucumbers to the vinegar mixture and toss well. Return to the platter in a single layer. Cover with plastic wrap and refrigerate for 3 to 4 hours.

Transfer to a serving dish and garnish with dill.

Quick-Braised Cucumbers
<u>AND</u> Radishes

1 tablespoon unsalted butter

1 tablespoon vegetable oil

1 pound radishes, halved

Kosher salt

1 pound Kirby cucumbers (about 3), quartered, cored, and cut into 2-inch lengths

2 teaspoons apple cider vinegar

¼ teaspoon chile flakes

Inspired by the soul food tradition of topping hot vegetables with cold pickles, I decided to try doing hot pickles. The first time I tasted these cooked cucumbers, I got my groove on with a happy dance. Guess what? Cucumbers taste amazing when they heat up in the pan and get doused with vinegar. They end up as tender as the radishes while keepin' their cool snap. Yum is right.

Heat the butter and oil in a large skillet over medium heat until the butter melts. Add the radishes and ½ teaspoon salt. Stir to coat the radishes, then cook, stirring occasionally, until the radishes are lightly browned at the edges, about 8 minutes.

Add the cucumbers and ¼ teaspoon salt. Cook, stirring often, until the cucumbers are just heated through and are the same texture as the radishes, about 3 minutes.

Stir in the vinegar, chile flakes, and 2 tablespoons water. Cook, stirring occasionally, until the water evaporates, about 1 minute. Serve hot.

Summer Squash ⏤AND⏤ Pesto Salad

½ cup fresh basil leaves

2 garlic cloves, smashed

2½ teaspoons kosher salt

¼ cup extra-virgin olive oil

4 small zucchini, quartered and cut into ½-inch slices

2 small yellow squash, quartered and cut into ½-inch slices

1 tablespoon minced fresh red chile

2 teaspoons fresh lemon zest

Mild summer squash takes on big punchy flavors—garlic, chile, lemon—in this superfast salad. Because gardens overflow with squash the same time basil plants are bloomin', I put the two together. To get all the goodness of basil pesto without the fuss, I just chop and mix everything on the cutting board. Saves me a bowl to clean and results in an aromatic sauce.

Combine the basil, garlic, ½ teaspoon salt, and half of the oil on a large cutting board. Chop into coarse bits, then add the remaining oil and chop and mix until everything is finely minced.

Toss the zucchini and squash with the remaining 2 teaspoons salt until evenly coated, then toss in the chile and lemon zest. Scatter on a platter and spoon the basil mixture on top. Serve immediately.

Seared Summer Squash <u>with</u> Sage

2 tablespoons plus 2
   teaspoons extra-virgin
   olive oil

2 large summer squash,
   trimmed and halved
   lengthwise

1 onion, thinly sliced

2 fresh sage leaves

Kosher salt

In Southern kitchens, the traditional way to bring out the sweetness in squash with no added sugar is to cook it nice and slow. To get that sweetness with the charred flavor I love, I sear the squash first. Then, I take my time with it, letting it get all floppy but not to the point where it's broken down into a mush. These slices end up silky soft with a woodsy scent from the sage. They're so buttery, sweet, and smooth, I could eat the whole pan by myself!

Heat a large cast-iron skillet over high heat. Rub 2 teaspoons of the oil all over the squash. When the skillet is smoking hot, put in the squash cut sides down. Let them sit, pressing lightly with a spatula, until seared and browned, 1 to 2 minutes. Flip and brown the curved side too, another minute or so. Transfer the squash to a cutting board. Turn off the heat, but leave the skillet on the stove.

When the squash are cool enough to handle, cut them into 1/4-inch-thick slices. Heat the remaining 2 tablespoons oil in the same skillet over medium heat. Add the onion and sage leaves and cook, stirring, for 1 minute. Add the squash and 1 teaspoon salt. Reduce the heat to medium-low and cook, stirring occasionally, until the squash are tender all the way through, 8 to 10 minutes. Serve hot.

Summer Squash [AND] Pepper Hash [WITH] Country Ham and Fried Eggs

SERVES 4	*Everyday*

3 cups ½-inch cubes zucchini and summer squash

3 tablespoons vegetable oil

Kosher salt

1 onion, finely diced

1 small green bell pepper, seeded and diced

½ cup finely diced country ham

1 Cubanelle pepper, seeded and thinly sliced

1 tablespoon minced fresh hot chile

1 teaspoon fresh thyme leaves

4 large eggs

Simple. Fast. Delicious. Summer squash replace potatoes in my take on a diner breakfast, complete with hash, ham, and eggs. Light and fresh, and they leave you feeling energized and ready for the day.

Toss the squash with 1 tablespoon of the oil and ¼ teaspoon salt in a large bowl. Heat a large cast-iron skillet over high heat. Add the squash in a single layer and cook, stirring occasionally, until lightly browned, about 2 minutes. Transfer to a plate.

Add 1 tablespoon of the remaining oil to the hot skillet, then add the onion. Cook, stirring occasionally, until just translucent, about 2 minutes. Add the bell pepper and country ham and cook, stirring often, until the pepper is crisp-tender, about 2 minutes. Add the Cubanelle pepper and chile and cook, stirring, for 1 minute. Fold the squash into the mixture and sprinkle with the thyme. Turn the heat to low to keep warm.

Heat the remaining 1 tablespoon oil in another large cast-iron skillet or a nonstick skillet over medium-high heat. Crack the eggs into the pan and fry to your desired doneness. I like my yolks runny, so I turn off the heat once the whites are set.

Divide the hash among four serving plates and slide a fried egg on top of each. Sprinkle the eggs lightly with salt and serve hot.

Red Pepper Bread Soup

SERVES 4	Everyday

1/4 cup extra-virgin olive oil, plus more for serving

1 large onion, finely diced

1 red bell pepper, seeded and finely diced

1 serrano chile, minced

6 garlic cloves, chopped

1 teaspoon sweet paprika

1/2 teaspoon ground cumin

1/2 teaspoon dried oregano

1/2 teaspoon ground ginger

1/8 teaspoon ground cardamom

1/8 teaspoon ground cinnamon

Kosher salt and freshly ground black pepper

1 cup finely chopped fresh cilantro with stems, plus more for serving

4 cups unsalted vegetable stock

1 teaspoon white wine vinegar

3 cups baguette cubes, toasted

When I got my DNA profile, I discovered that I share genetic ancestry with people living in Portugal. I guess that explains my love of olive oil and Mediterranean spices! One Portuguese dish that shares the soul food spirit of not wasting food is migas, also known as açorda. It's a soup that uses up stale bread. Vegetable stock is seasoned with sautéed onion and pepper, then spices, then lots of cilantro. Just before serving, bread is folded in, creating a hearty stew consistency. It can be eaten alone or served alongside grilled chicken or fish for a simple dinner.

Heat the oil in a large Dutch oven or saucepan over high heat. Add the onion, bell pepper, and chile. Cook, stirring occasionally, until seared at the edges and the onion is almost translucent, about 5 minutes. You want to char the vegetables to get their depth of flavor. Add the garlic, paprika, cumin, oregano, ginger, cardamom, cinnamon, 1 teaspoon salt, and 1/2 teaspoon black pepper. Cook, stirring, for 1 minute. Stir in the cilantro, then add the stock and vinegar. Bring to a boil, then lower the heat to maintain a simmer. Simmer until the vegetables are tender, about 30 minutes.

Stir in 1/4 teaspoon salt, then fold in the bread. Divide among serving bowls and garnish with cilantro. Drizzle with oil and serve.

I call salt compliments because
if you don't use it, you AIN'T GON'
GIT NO COMPLIMENTS.

Red Cabbage <small>AND</small> Beet Slaw <small>WITH</small> Horseradish-Ginger Dressing

SERVES 6

Everyday & Celebration

1 tablespoon grated peeled fresh horseradish

1 teaspoon grated peeled fresh ginger

1 teaspoon freshly grated lemon zest

1 cup mayonnaise

2 tablespoons fresh lemon juice

Kosher salt and freshly ground black pepper

2 cups finely diced green cabbage

2 cups finely diced red cabbage

2 cups coarsely grated peeled red beet

Snipped fresh chives, for garnish

We celebrate Juneteenth with red foods (see page 304), so this is the slaw I'm bringing to my picnic. Red cabbage and beets taste light and lemony in my horseradish-ginger dressing. I toss green cabbage into the mix, too, for a medley of bright crunch.

Whisk the horseradish, ginger, lemon zest, mayonnaise, lemon juice, 1/2 teaspoon salt, and 1/2 teaspoon black pepper in a large bowl. Add both cabbages and the beet and fold until well mixed. Season with salt and pepper. Garnish with chives and serve.

Make ahead: The slaw can be refrigerated for up to 2 days. Before serving, toss again and top with snipped chives.

Roasted Cauliflower WITH Raisins AND Lemon-Pepper Millet

1 cup millet

1 bay leaf

Kosher salt and freshly ground black pepper

1 large (1½-pound) cauliflower, cut into ½-inch pieces

3 tablespoons canola oil

1 lemon

¼ cup golden raisins

¼ cup chopped fresh flat-leaf parsley

Teeny golden millet seeds taste like corn and cashews had a love child. Sweet and nutty, they're awesome with so many different seasonings. In Africa, where they're thought to have originated and where they're a staple, they're often eaten alone, simmered into a porridge or baked into bread. I play up their sweetness by tossing in caramelized cauliflower and raisins, then balance it with the bite of lots of black pepper and parsley. Child, a bowl of this is dinner enough for me. But you can have it with some nice grilled chicken or fish too.

You can skip the cauliflower for a quick millet pilaf with the raisins and parsley. Season to taste with salt, pepper, and lemon juice. Or you can forget the millet for a yummy pan of roasted lemony cauliflower.

Preheat the oven to 425°F.

Pour the millet into a large saucepan and set over medium heat. Toast, shaking the pan occasionally, until golden brown and fragrant, about 15 minutes. Add the bay leaf, 2 cups water, and ¾ teaspoon salt and bring to a boil over high heat. Cover, reduce the heat to low, and cook until the millet is just tender and the water is absorbed, about 10 minutes. Let stand for 5 minutes.

Meanwhile, toss the cauliflower, oil, ¾ teaspoon salt, and ½ teaspoon pepper on a half-sheet pan until evenly coated. Roast until well browned, about 15 minutes. Zest the lemon directly over the hot cauliflower. Cut the lemon in half and squeeze the juice from one half over the vegetables.

Fluff the millet in the saucepan with a fork to separate the grains, then scrape the cauliflower into the millet and add the raisins and parsley. Fold until well mixed. Season to taste with salt, pepper, and more lemon juice.

Broccoli Slaw WITH Pecans AND Raisins

Everyday & Celebration

1 cup mayonnaise

¼ cup apple cider vinegar

⅓ cup buttermilk

2 tablespoons drained bottled horseradish

½ teaspoon cayenne pepper

1 teaspoon kosher salt

½ teaspoon freshly ground black pepper

2 large heads broccoli

2 carrots, peeled and grated

½ red onion, thinly sliced

⅓ cup raisins

3 tablespoons sunflower seeds, toasted

⅓ cup pecans, toasted and coarsely chopped

Lordy, there's not a cookout in the South without a bowl of broccoli slaw sweating on the picnic table. Green florets drowning in sugared mayonnaise, plopped onto plates cozying up with cornbread and ribs. My version's lighter than the ones I remember from my childhood. The dressing's neither sweet nor thick, but bright with horseradish and vinegar. It coats the broccoli, carrots, and onion the way peppers get slicked with hot pepper vinegar. To give the slaw cravable crunch, I toss on the toasted nuts and seeds right before serving. You can even leave them on the table for folks to serve themselves.

Combine the mayonnaise, vinegar, buttermilk, horseradish, cayenne, salt, and black pepper in a pint jar. Screw on the lid and shake until very well mixed.

Cut the stems from the broccoli and cut off the peel with a sharp knife. Cut the peeled stems into very thin slices. Cut the florets into small pieces. Toss with the carrots, onion, raisins, and 1 cup dressing in a large bowl until well mixed.

Right before serving, stir in the sunflower seeds and pecans. Transfer to a serving bowl and serve with the remaining dressing.

Pan-Roasted Cabbage <small>AND</small> Celery Root

Everyday

1 tablespoon plus 1 teaspoon extra-virgin olive oil

2 cups finely diced cabbage

1½ cups diced peeled celery root

½ onion, finely chopped

2 garlic cloves, chopped

¼ teaspoon chile flakes

Kosher salt

1 teaspoon apple cider vinegar

When I think about how my ancestors ate, I remind myself that vegetables don't grow in the winter. People relied on what they kept in the cellar those cold months—roots and crucifers. I also think about how wood fires warmed their kitchens and imagine the smoky flavor they must've gotten in their cast-iron pans. So I start this dish by charring cabbage and celery root. It brings out their natural earthy sweetness quickly, making this is a fast side dish you can whip up all year round.

Heat a large cast-iron skillet over high heat. Add 1 tablespoon of the oil and swirl to coat the bottom of the pan. Add the cabbage and celery root and cook, stirring often, until browned in spots, about 3 minutes. Push the vegetables to one side of the skillet.

Add the remaining 1 teaspoon oil to the other side of the skillet along with the onion. Cook, stirring occasionally, until lightly browned, about 1 minute. Add the garlic and stir everything together. Sprinkle with the chile flakes and ½ teaspoon salt and stir again. Stir in the vinegar, transfer to a serving dish, and serve immediately.

Smashed Carrots ᴡɪᴛʜ Curry Oil

SERVES 4	Everyday

3 tablespoons vegetable oil

½ teaspoon Curry Powder (page 242) or store-bought mild yellow curry powder

1 pound carrots, scrubbed

Kosher salt

Juice of 1 lemon

Smashing baked carrots cracks open crevices, ideal for soaking up a super-easy curry oil. This is so easy, but it's sooo good.

Preheat the oven to 375°F. Line a half-sheet pan with parchment paper.

Mix 2 tablespoons of the oil with the curry powder in a small bowl and let stand.

Rub the remaining 1 tablespoon oil all over the carrots and sprinkle with salt. Bake until tender, about 45 minutes.

Sprinkle the lemon juice all over the carrots and return to the oven. Bake for 15 minutes longer.

Transfer the carrots to a serving plate. With a large spatula, gently press each carrot until smashed and flattened a bit. Drizzle the curry oil all over. Serve hot, warm, or at room temperature.

Roasted Whole Carrots <u>WITH</u> Benne

2 pounds thin carrots, peeled

2 teaspoons extra-virgin olive oil

$\frac{1}{2}$ teaspoon kosher salt

2 tablespoons Lemon-Thyme Benne (page 244)

To celebrate seasonal carrots, I roast them whole when they're slim and sweet during their peak harvest. This dish is still tasty with fatter carrots cut into thinner sticks, thanks to the crunchy topping. Benne seeds, flecked with thyme and lemon zest, coat the caramelized roots with a pippity-poppy crunch.

Preheat the oven to 450°F.

Toss the carrots, oil, and salt on a half-sheet pan until evenly coated. Spread the carrots in a single layer.

Roast until browned and tender, 20 to 25 minutes, flipping once halfway through cooking. Transfer to a serving platter and top with the benne.

Make ahead: The roasted carrots without the topping can be refrigerated for up to 3 days. I like leftovers at room temperature or even cold, but you can reheat them before sprinkling on the benne.

Parsnips ☰WITH Honey-Orange Glaze

SERVES 4	*Everyday*

1¹/₂ pounds parsnips, peeled and quartered lengthwise, cored if necessary

2 tablespoons extra-virgin olive oil

Kosher salt and freshly ground black pepper

¹/₂ cup fresh orange juice

1 tablespoon raw honey

1 tablespoon apple cider vinegar

1 cinnamon stick

1 whole clove

Chopped fresh flat-leaf parsley, for serving

I like the bitter edge of parsnips against this citrus honey glaze. To make sure the parsnips don't end up too bitter, you need to see if they have a fibrous core. Young slender parsnips tend not to. Fat older ones have a woody center that needs to be cut out. After quartering them lengthwise, slice out the tough part.

Preheat the oven to 450°F.

Toss the parsnips with the oil and ¹/₂ teaspoon salt on a half-sheet pan. Spread in a single layer and grind pepper on top. Roast, flipping once, until tender, about 30 minutes.

Meanwhile, combine the orange juice, honey, vinegar, cinnamon, clove, and ¹/₄ teaspoon salt and bring to a boil in a small saucepan over high heat. Boil until syrupy, about 5 minutes. Remove from the heat and reserve.

Pour the syrup all over the parsnips and toss to coat. Top with parsley and serve.

Smashed Beets <u>with</u> Red Onion <u>and</u> Mint

Everyday & *Celebration*

6 beets (2 pounds), scrubbed

1/2 red onion, very thinly sliced

4 teaspoons red wine vinegar

2 tablespoons plus 2 teaspoons extra-virgin olive oil

Kosher salt and freshly ground black pepper

Torn fresh mint leaves, for serving

When I go home to Nashville, I don't recognize half the city. Hot restaurants, trendy coffee shops, and tall apartment buildings keep popping up. One newish restaurant I like is Rolf and Daughters. On my last visit, they served a smashed beet with yogurt sauce. I fell hard for that beet. When smashed, it almost melts in your mouth. The normally meaty texture goes silky. I experimented with the same at home and wanted to let the smashed beet show off, so I gave it a simple oil-and-vinegar drizzle. The onion adds a bright crunch and the mint freshness, but the beets don't even need them.

Preheat the oven to 400°F.

Wrap each beet in foil and place on a half-sheet pan. Bake until tender enough for a knife to slide through easily, about 1 hour.

Meanwhile, toss the onion, vinegar, oil, 1 teaspoon salt, and 1/2 teaspoon pepper in a small bowl. Let stand until ready to serve.

Rub the skins off the hot beets, then cut large beets in half. Using your palm or a spatula, gently smash into 1/2-inch-thick disks. Transfer to serving plates and top with the onion mixture, drizzling the vinaigrette all around. Scatter the mint leaves on top. Serve hot, warm, or at room temperature.

Barbecued Celery Root

SERVES 6	*Everyday & Celebration*

2 small celery roots, trimmed, peeled, and cut into ¾-inch-thick rounds

Extra-virgin olive oil, for brushing

Kosher salt

Barbecue Sauce (page 245)

If it looks like barbecue and smells like barbecue—well, then, that's what it is. And it's so delicious! I cut celery root into steaks, then grill them and glaze them with barbecue sauce. The vegetable gets juicy and smoky and almost meaty. When you cut into it with a fork and knife, it feels like a proper main dish, not just a side disguised as one. This one's for all those vegetarians at the cookout, and especially for my husband, Matthew.

Heat a grill to medium heat.

Score both sides of the celery root rounds in a diamond pattern with the tip of a sharp paring knife. Brush a thin coating of oil all over the rounds, then sprinkle with salt.

Place the slices on the hot grill grate. Cover and grill, turning occasionally, until the roots are just tender, about 45 minutes. A sharp knife or a cake tester should slide through with a little resistance.

Uncover the grill and brush the celery roots with barbecue sauce. Grill, turning and brushing, until the sauce has caramelized and charred in spots, about 5 minutes. Serve hot with more sauce on the side.

Curried Mushroom ⦿ Coconut Soup

SERVES 6	Everyday

2 tablespoons extra-virgin olive oil

2 tablespoons unsalted butter

12 ounces portobello mushrooms (ribs scraped out), cut into $1/2$-inch pieces (6 cups)

6 ounces shiitake mushrooms (stems removed), very thinly sliced (3 cups)

1 celery stalk, chopped

1 onion, chopped

1 leek, white and light green parts only, chopped

4 garlic cloves, sliced

$1/4$ teaspoon cayenne pepper

Kosher salt and freshly ground black pepper

2 teaspoons curry powder

3 cups unsalted vegetable broth

1 cup coconut milk

Lime wedges, for serving

Throughout Africa and its diaspora, from South Africa to Jamaica, curry pops up everywhere. And it's no wonder. One of the largest populations of Indian immigrants resides in South Africa. When they first arrived, they brought their spices and know-how and bam! Before you know it, curry makes its way to American soul food.

And it holds a special place in my heart. When my husband, Matthew, and I first met, he cooked chicken curry for me. I was so impressed (it was delicious!), I decided to stick with him. Now that he doesn't eat meat, I've created this dish for him. It's got all the spiciness of our first-date dish without any of the meat, plus it's got creaminess from the coconut milk and a nice zing with a squirt of lime juice.

Heat the oil and butter in a large pot over medium-high heat until the butter melts. Add the mushrooms and cook, stirring occasionally, until browned and the liquid has released and then evaporated, 5 to 6 minutes. Stir in the celery, onion, leek, garlic, cayenne, $1^1/2$ teaspoons salt, and $1/2$ teaspoon pepper. Cook, stirring often, until the onion is translucent, about 3 minutes. Stir in the curry powder.

Add the broth and bring to a boil over high heat. Reduce the heat to maintain a simmer and simmer until the vegetables are tender, about 30 minutes. Stir in the coconut milk and cook until heated through. Season to taste with salt and pepper. Serve hot with lime wedges.

Make ahead: The soup can be refrigerated for up to 5 days. Reheat before serving.

We share a heritage, culture, and spirit in the African-American community. But we're not all the same. In the food world—and the world at large—that's a struggle. One thing that has been passed down to us all? The welcome gene. Hospitality is in our blood. You never leave someone's home empty-handed or sit down at someone's table without being fed. Even if it's at the table of a restaurant that hasn't opened yet. In Birmingham, I chatted with chef Roscoe Hall II at Fero, chef Akhtar Nawab's Italian restaurant. Roscoe's the director of operations for all of Akhtar's Birmingham restaurants, and he took the time to sit with me a few days before the opening.

While we talked, his team kept sending out plate after plate. The one that really blew me away combined potato gnocchi with pickled mustard seeds. That revelation led me to pickling mustard seeds for my spin on potato salad (see page 103). More important than the food were the stories Roscoe shared of his struggles finding his place in the food industry.

Roscoe grew up in Chicago, the son of an ex–Black Panther, the grandson of a legendary barbecue restaurant owner. He says, "We're roots as hell. We bleed barbecue sauce." Roscoe's also into punk rock. And he likes to make kimchi pimento cheese. He doesn't conform to any stereotype. Everywhere he's lived—San Francisco, Savannah, Portland—it's been hard to have people accept him just for who he is. Or not to mistake him for another black chef. Even if that other dude doesn't look anything like him! (And no, Roscoe and I are not related.)

To make sure the next generation doesn't have to deal with what he's gone through, he mentors younger chefs. Roscoe says, "I want to show kids in the 'hood how to mirepoix." And he wants to show them that they can be themselves and be successful in the restaurant industry. It's another way of showing true hospitality.

Smashed Red Potatoes WITH Mustard Mayonnaise Drizzle

Everyday & Celebration

6 medium red potatoes (2 pounds), scrubbed

1 tablespoon extra-virgin olive oil

1 tablespoon apple cider vinegar

4 teaspoons yellow mustard seeds

1 1/2 teaspoons kosher salt

1/4 cup mayonnaise

2 teaspoons Dijon mustard

Snipped fresh chives, for serving

Potato salad's the essential soul food side dish. I cherish it in all its forms, but I wanted to show off the potatoes here. (Sometimes, they get a little lost in the glop.) I bake red potatoes—freshly dug summer ones are the best—until they're soft enough to smash. Without any salt, they taste earthy and sweet and feel creamy and fluffy. A little mustard-mayonnaise drizzle will give you all the cookout memories.

Preheat the oven to 375°F. Line a half-sheet pan with parchment paper.

Rub the potatoes with the oil and place on the prepared pan in a single layer. Bake until tender enough for a knife to slide through easily, about 1 hour.

Meanwhile, combine the vinegar, mustard seeds, 1 cup water, and 1/2 teaspoon salt in a small saucepan and bring to a boil over high heat. Reduce the heat to medium and simmer until the seeds have doubled in size, about 10 minutes. Remove from the heat and pour through a sieve into a bowl. Reserve the seeds and cooking liquid.

Whisk the mayonnaise, mustard, mustard seeds, 3 tablespoons reserved cooking liquid, and the remaining 1 teaspoon salt in a small bowl.

Gently smash the hot potatoes into 1/2-inch-thick disks. Transfer to a serving plate and drizzle with the mustard sauce. Garnish with chives and serve hot or warm.

Curried Sweet Potato Salad

Everyday & Celebration

6 cups 1-inch chunks peeled sweet potatoes

Kosher salt

¼ cup mayonnaise

¼ cup sour cream

3 tablespoons finely chopped bread & butter pickles

2 teaspoons Curry Powder (page 242) or store-bought mild yellow curry powder

1 teaspoon apple cider vinegar

2 large eggs, hard-boiled (see page 15), peeled, and diced

1 small red, yellow, or orange bell pepper, seeded and finely diced

1 small green bell pepper, seeded and finely diced

Sliced scallions, for garnish

Sweet potatoes pack so much more fiber and flavor than plain ol' potatoes, they deserve to star in this summer salad. Crunchy with peppers and creamy with a curried dressing, this side dish would work well with any grilled meat or vegetables.

Garnet, jewel, and Beauregard yams taste best in this salad. They're actually sweet potatoes but they're called yams. Don't ask me why. All I know is that their dark orange flesh is sweeter and smoother than others.

Put the sweet potatoes in a large saucepan and add enough cold water to cover by 2 inches. Very generously salt the water and bring to a boil over high heat. Boil until the sweet potatoes are tender, about 15 minutes. Drain well, then spread out on a half-sheet pan to quickly cool to room temperature.

Meanwhile, whisk the mayonnaise, sour cream, pickles, curry powder, vinegar, and ¾ teaspoon salt in a large bowl. Add the eggs, both bell peppers, and the cooled sweet potatoes. Fold gently until well mixed.

You can serve the salad right away, but it's better if it's covered and chilled for at least an hour or two for the flavors to meld. When ready to serve, sprinkle the scallions on top.

Make ahead: The salad can be refrigerated for up to 2 days.

Sweet Potato Pudding ⎯WITH⎯ Clementines

Celebration

3 pounds sweet potatoes
  (about 3 large)

1/2 cup packed brown sugar

1/4 cup extra-virgin olive oil

2 tablespoons molasses

Zest and juice of
  1 clementine

1 teaspoon kosher salt

Maldon flaky sea salt,
  for sprinkling

A little sweetness is a signature of soul cooking. Breaking straight-up savory courses with a cup of this silky citrus-scented pudding will make the whole meal happier. Olive oil keeps these sweet potatoes from tipping into a full-on dessert, but swap in butter and top with whipped cream and you've got a new dessert recipe too!

Preheat the oven to 375°F. Line a half-sheet pan with foil.

Put the sweet potatoes on the prepared half-sheet pan and bake until very soft, 1 to 1 1/2 hours.

Whisk the brown sugar, oil, molasses, clementine zest and juice, and kosher salt in a large bowl. Peel the potatoes and pass through a food mill or ricer into the bowl. Fold until well mixed. Divide among cups, sprinkle with flaky salt, and serve hot or warm.

Creamy Buttermilk Mashed Potatoes

SERVES 6 | *Celebration*

3 pounds medium russet
   potatoes (about 5),
   scrubbed and each cut
   into 8 even pieces

Kosher salt

1 cup whole milk, warmed

8 tablespoons (4 ounces)
   unsalted butter, cut up
   and softened

¼ cup buttermilk

A little tangy buttermilk turns regular mashed potatoes into a *hot-dang!* dish. You know I like that pucker. The other secret to my spuds? Lots of milk. The mix may look thin, but trust me, it'll stiffen as it sits, so you don't want to start too thick.

Put the potatoes in a large saucepan and add enough cold water to cover by 2 inches. Very generously salt the water. Make it as salty as the sea! Bring to a boil over high heat, then cover the pan and reduce the heat to low. Simmer until the potatoes are very soft, about 30 minutes.

Drain the potatoes, then put them through a food mill or ricer into a large bowl. Immediately fold in the milk and butter until smooth, then fold in the buttermilk. Season with salt. I found 2 teaspoons to be the right amount. Serve hot.

Cassava ⎯WITH⎯ Coconut Milk ⎯AND⎯ Lime

SERVES 6	*Everyday*

3 pounds cassava

Kosher salt

1 tablespoon unsalted
butter

1 onion, finely chopped

2 garlic cloves, minced

1 tablespoon minced peeled
fresh ginger

1 cup coconut milk

Zest and juice of 1 lime,
plus 1 lime for serving

1/2 cup coconut cream

1 jalapeño chile, thinly
sliced

1/4 cup unsweetened
coconut flakes, toasted

Mmm mmm, this is one big bowl of comfort. Cassava is the starchy tuber that tapioca comes from. When it's cooked and mashed, and, in this case, mixed with coconut milk, it becomes super-creamy. When you bite into a chunk of cassava, it goes from sweet outside to earthy center. I first got the idea for this recipe from a chef in Kenya. But as I found out more about cassava, I realized that it journeyed with my people, from West Africa through the Caribbean to these shores. I've taken the flavors here on the same journey.

Cassava, also known as yuca or manioc, looks like tree branches, with a dark brown rough skin. Young cassava is less likely to have any rot and will be sweeter and less starchy. Look for thin, small cassava with an unblemished surface. When you cut it, discard any parts with black lines in the white flesh. Since you can't see that from the outside, buy more than you need for this recipe.

Trim the top and bottom of the cassava, then cut into thirds from top to bottom. Use a sharp knife to cut all the peel off the pieces, including any purple parts near the skin. You should be left with only white flesh. Cut the flesh into 1 1/2-inch chunks.

Bring a large saucepan of water to a boil. Add the cassava and 1 teaspoon salt. Reduce the heat to maintain a steady boil and cook until tender, about 20 minutes. Reserve 1/2 cup of the cooking liquid. Pour the rest of the cooking liquid out of the pan, leaving the cassava in the pan. Mash the cassava coarsely, leaving big chunks in the mix.

Melt the butter in a medium saucepan over medium-high heat. Add the onion and 3/4 teaspoon salt and cook, stirring, for 3 minutes. Add the garlic and ginger and cook, stirring often, until the onion is tender, about 4 minutes. Add the coconut milk, reserved cooking water, and lime zest. Stir well and simmer for 5 minutes. Add the lime juice and simmer for 1 minute. Add the coconut cream and bring to a simmer.

Pour the coconut mixture over the cassava and fold until well mixed. Divide among serving bowls. Zest the remaining lime over the cassava, then top with the jalapeño slices and coconut flakes. Cut the zested lime into wedges and serve with the hot cassava.

Sorghum ⏤ WITH ⏤ Butternut Squash, Onion, Celery, ⏤ AND ⏤ Toasted Pumpkin Seeds

SERVES 4   *Everyday & Celebration*

1 cup sorghum

Kosher salt and freshly
  ground black pepper

2 tablespoons extra-virgin
  olive oil

1/2 cup finely diced onion

1/2 cup finely diced celery

2 garlic cloves, minced

2 cups finely diced
  butternut squash

1 teaspoon chopped fresh
  thyme leaves

2 teaspoons red wine
  vinegar

1/4 cup finely chopped fresh
  flat-leaf parsley

2 tablespoons pumpkin
  seeds, toasted

Sorghum came to these shores on slave ships from West Africa, both as food for the enslaved during the Middle Passage and as a crop to be transplanted. It's largely been forgotten for years. If it's used in cooking at all, it's as a syrup. But I'm bringing back this ancient cereal grain here. It has a nuttiness and chewiness that pair so well with earthy and tender butternut squash. This gluten-free grain salad is a sitting salad, nice for toting to potlucks and picnics.

Combine the sorghum, 3 cups water, and 1 tablespoon salt in a large saucepan and bring to a boil over high heat. Cover, reduce the heat to low, and simmer until tender, about 50 minutes. Drain if necessary.

Heat the oil in a large, deep skillet over medium-high heat. Add the onion, celery, garlic, 3/4 teaspoon salt, and 1/4 teaspoon pepper. Cook, stirring, for 2 minutes. Add the squash and cook, stirring, for 2 minutes. Add the thyme and cook, stirring, for 3 minutes. Stir in the vinegar and cook until it evaporates. The vegetables should be browned and soft.

Add the sorghum and stir until heated through. Fold in the parsley and remove from the heat. Transfer to a serving dish and top with the pumpkin seeds. Serve hot, warm, or at room temperature.

Kelewele: Marinated Fried Plantains

1 (14.5-ounce) can fire-roasted diced tomatoes

2 teaspoons grated peeled fresh ginger

½ teaspoon chile flakes

Kosher salt

3 large ripe plantains

Vegetable oil, for frying

Come with me to Ghana . . . by way of London. That's where I first tasted this West African specialty. I had fried plantains before, but kelewele starts with a tomato marinade. It leaves ginger bits clinging to the browned outside surrounding the banana-like center. And makes the plantains tangy and spicy and oh so good. As a newly arrived runway model in that foggy town, I was welcomed by friends of friends who were all Ghanaian. When they cooked this dish for me, they sat me at the table like family. I felt so at home, as if kelewele had been a part of my life all along. Turns out, it has! Recently, I found out that my ancestry traces back to Ghana. Whether or not kelewele runs in your blood, you'll love it as much as I do.

Be sure to buy plantains that are completely black but not too soft. Soft ones are on the verge of rotting and have a funk you don't want.

Mix the tomatoes, ginger, chile flakes, and ½ teaspoon salt in a large bowl. Peel the plantains, halve them lengthwise, and cut into ½-inch slices at an angle. Add to the tomato mixture and turn to evenly coat. Cover with plastic wrap and let stand for 1 hour at room temperature.

Fill a large cast-iron skillet with oil to a depth of ¼ inch. Heat over medium-high heat until shimmering. Add enough plantains to fit in a single layer without crowding. You can pick them out of the marinade and wipe off any big bits with your fingers. Fry, flipping once, until browned and tender, about 3 minutes. Drain on paper towels. Repeat with the remaining plantains. Discard the marinade. Serve hot.

Watermelon WITH Mint AND Lime

Everyday & Celebration

1 tablespoon kosher salt

1 tablespoon freshly grated lime zest

1 tablespoon minced fresh mint leaves

1 small watermelon, trimmed and cut into 1-inch-thick wedges

Watermelon ain't what it used to be. Anyone of certain generations can tell you that. And this isn't just another "I walked eight miles in the snow" yarn. It's a fact. Long story short: commercial growers bred out the big black seeds to make the fruit easier to eat and lost some of its sweetness and soul in the process. There are small farmers and home growers out there trying to revive heirloom watermelons and bring back the complex juiciness of the good ol' fruit. Until I can easily get my hands on one, I do the best I can with what the supermarket's got.

To bring out the sugars in the red flesh—and mimic the layers of flavors I remember from childhood—I sprinkle wedges with this lime and mint salt. A bit of salt actually makes the fruit sweeter, the lime adds floral tartness, and mint makes it extra refreshing. You can double or triple the mix if you're cutting up a few melons for a party.

Rub the salt, lime zest, and mint together in a small bowl with your fingers until very well mixed. When ready to serve, arrange the watermelon on a platter and sprinkle with the salt mixture.

Watermelon Salad <u>with</u> Radishes

Everyday & Celebration

Kosher salt and freshly ground black pepper

1 bunch red radishes, cut into 1/8-inch slices

2 tablespoons red wine vinegar

4 teaspoons extra-virgin olive oil

1/2 red onion, cut into thin slivers

4 1/2 pounds watermelon (1/4 of a large melon), rind removed, flesh cut into 1-inch cubes

2 tablespoons torn mint leaves

If your watermelon isn't very sweet, force it to be savory. That's what I've done by adding the peppery bite of radishes and onion and a three-ingredient vinaigrette. With mint strewn all over the juicy fruit, this whole salad ends up being super-refreshing.

Dissolve a spoonful of salt in a large bowl of ice and water. Add the radishes and let sit for a few minutes to crisp.

Whisk the vinegar, oil, and 1 teaspoon salt in a large bowl. Drain the radishes and add to the bowl, along with the onion and watermelon. Gently toss with your hands to coat evenly.

Spread on a serving platter, grind pepper all over, and top with the mint.

Beans

Black-Eyed Pea Salad <u>WITH</u> Hot Sauce Vinaigrette

SERVES 4 | *Everyday & Celebration*

2 garlic cloves, grated on a Microplane

2 tablespoons apple cider vinegar

1 tablespoon yellow mustard

1 tablespoon hot sauce

1 teaspoon honey

Kosher salt and freshly ground black pepper

6 tablespoons vegetable oil

1 (15-ounce) can black-eyed peas, rinsed and drained

2 mini cucumbers, cut into $1/2$-inch dice

$1/2$ sweet onion, finely chopped

1 pint cherry tomatoes or grape tomatoes, halved

$1/4$ cup picked fresh dill

When I say black-eyed peas have a long history, I mean long. More than five thousand years ago, they were domesticated in West Africa. The crop spread throughout the continent, then traveled in slave ship holds to America. In the Carolinas, slaves planted black-eyed peas in the same way they had back home—along edges of fields to keep down weeds and enrich the soil. That's why they're sometimes called cowpeas and field peas. Originally eaten only by slaves, black-eyed peas became a part of all Southerners' meals. But they hold a special significance in the heart of every African-American. We eat them for good luck on New Year's in a rice dish known as hoppin' John. That tradition comes from a long history of black-eyed peas symbolizing luck and prosperity in Africa, where they're part of spiritual ceremonies too. They're a part of our culinary DNA. And they're delicious.

Black-eyed peas are tender, skin to center, and this helps them soak up sauces. Because they're nice and mild, I drench them with a hot sauce dressing, honeyed yet sharp with garlic and mustard. In this salad, cucumbers and onion balance the peas' creaminess with crunch, and tomatoes burst juiciness. Down South, we call this a sitting salad. It can sit on the summer picnic table without wilting, so it's the perfect potluck dish. Get ready for this salad to become one of your favorites.

Whisk the garlic, vinegar, mustard, hot sauce, honey, $1/4$ teaspoon salt, and $1/4$ teaspoon pepper in a large bowl until smooth. While whisking, add the oil in a slow, steady stream. Whisk until emulsified.

Add the peas, cucumbers, onion, tomatoes, dill, and $1/2$ teaspoon salt. Toss until well mixed. You can serve this right away or let it sit at room temperature for up to 1 hour.

Make ahead: The salad can be refrigerated for up to 1 day.

Quick-Cooked Red Beans

SERVES 6	*Everyday*

1 pound dried red beans, picked over for stones and rinsed

1 habanero chile, split

6 garlic cloves, peeled and gently smashed

3 sprigs fresh thyme

1 bay leaf

1 teaspoon apple cider vinegar

Kosher salt

Cooking at events feels like a race. I go as fast as I can, keeping an eye on the clock, knowing I'm outta time. For an event in Colorado, I didn't have enough hours to soak my red beans, so I just boiled them hard and hoped for the best. They turned out so tender and creamy! And that cooking liquid turned into a silky bean gravy that everyone slurped up. You'll want to do the same here.

Combine the beans, chile, garlic, thyme, bay leaf, and 4 quarts water in a large saucepan. Bring to a boil over high heat. Boil for 1 hour. If there isn't enough water to cover the beans after that hour, add more, 1/2 cup at a time.

Reduce the heat to maintain a steady simmer. Stir in the vinegar and 2 teaspoons salt. Simmer until the beans are tender and creamy, about 20 minutes. If the beans are old, they'll take longer. Discard the chile, thyme, and bay leaf. Season to taste with salt. Serve hot.

Make ahead: The beans can be refrigerated for up to 1 week. Reheat before serving.

White Beans ⫿WITH⫿ Caramelized Onions ⫿AND⫿ Smoked Salt

SERVES 6

Everyday

1 pound dried great northern beans or other small white beans, picked over, rinsed, and drained

1 small onion, finely chopped

4 garlic cloves, sliced

1½ teaspoons smoked salt, or more to taste

¼ teaspoon celery seeds

¼ teaspoon chile flakes

1 tablespoon extra-virgin olive oil

Finely chopped fresh parsley, for serving

I love, love, *love* beans. Almost as much as Mama hates them. She had 'em for dinner every night when she was away at boarding school. The school couldn't afford meat, so beans were the protein, slapped onto plates with scoops of sweet potatoes. That was some nasty stuff. She'd tell me about those miserable meals of pasty, tasteless beans to show me how lucky we were to have meat on our dinner table.

Years later, when I learned how to cook beans properly, I discovered that they're nothing at all like school cafeteria slop. Only problem was they took hours—and soaking overnight—to get 'em to a creamy comfort as warm as a big ol' hug. But I've managed to get hard-as-pebble beans *mmm mmm* tasty and tender in a fraction of the time with my quick soak and simmer technique. (You're welcome!) Smoked salt, now widely available on store shelves, gives the silky white beans a deep smokiness with no need for ham hocks or bacon. Sprinkling the salt like fairy dust into the simmer highlights the natural sweetness of the onion and garlic and the fresh bite from celery seeds and parsley.

I like to eat these creamy beans plain or with a side of collard greens and cornbread. If I have any left over, I make it the base of a soup, tossing in greens, tomatoes, stock, and anything else that looks good in my fridge.

Tip: If you know a day ahead of time that you want beans, soak the dried picked-over beans in cold water overnight and skip the first step.

Place the beans in a large saucepan and cover with cold water by 2 inches. Bring to a boil over high heat and boil hard for 40 minutes. Replenish the water if it falls below the beans. Drain well and return to the saucepan.

Cover the beans with cold water by 2 inches and bring to a boil. Reduce the heat to low and simmer for 10 minutes. Stir in the onion and garlic and simmer, swirling the saucepan occasionally, until the beans are tender enough to be smashed with the back of a spoon, about 25 minutes.

Stir in the smoked salt, celery seeds, and chile flakes. For a thicker stew consistency, smash or puree some beans using a fork or an immersion blender. Stir in the oil and top with the parsley. Serve hot.

Make ahead: The beans can be refrigerated for up to 1 week. Reheat before serving.

Creamy White Bean Soup
with Coconut and Chile

SERVES 6	Everyday

1 pound dried great
    northern beans or other
    small white beans,
    picked over, rinsed, and
    drained

1 onion, finely diced

1 carrot, finely diced

1 small celery stalk, finely
    diced

1 hot red chile, seeded and
    finely diced

1 garlic clove, minced

1 bay leaf

1/8 teaspoon cayenne
    pepper

Kosher salt

1 tablespoon coconut oil

I've got the African diaspora on my mind. When I'm in the kitchen, I try to imagine what my great-great-great-grandmother would make today with the ingredients we have. Foods moved with the slaves from the shores of West Africa to the Carolinas to the Caribbean. Our ancestors incorporated the seasonings and ingredients they encountered along the way. So I've taken beans to the Caribbean by simmering them with chile and bay leaf and finishing them with coconut. It's very important to add the coconut oil at the very end so its tropical flavor doesn't cook out. You want that nutty note in this steamy soup.

Put the beans in a large saucepan and add enough cold water to cover by 2 inches. Bring to a boil over high heat. Boil for 40 minutes, adding more water as needed to keep the beans covered by at least 1 inch.

Drain well, then return the beans to the pot. Add the onion, carrot, celery, chile, garlic, and bay leaf. Add enough water to cover all the solids by 2 inches. Bring to a boil over high heat, then reduce the heat to maintain a steady simmer. Simmer until the beans are soft enough to mash with a spoon, about 1 hour. The solids need to be covered by water—but only barely—in this stage. Add more water if anything peeps over the top, but otherwise, leave it be.

Stir in the cayenne and salt to taste. I like about 2 teaspoons salt. Mash half of the beans to thicken the cooking broth and to turn the whole thing into a light soup. Stir in the coconut oil until it melts. Season to taste with salt and serve right away.

Make ahead: The soup can be refrigerated for up to 1 week. Reheat before serving.

Mustard Seed–Marinated White <small>AND</small> Pinto Beans

Everyday

2 tablespoons red wine vinegar

2 teaspoons minced garlic

2 teaspoons yellow mustard seeds

½ teaspoon chile flakes

1 teaspoon kosher salt

½ teaspoon coarsely ground black pepper

½ cup extra-virgin olive oil

1 (15-ounce) can cannellini beans, rinsed and drained

1 (15-ounce) can pinto beans, rinsed and drained

Beans soak up a garlic-mustard vinaigrette in this superfast side dish. Because the skins toughen in the marinade, this is best made with canned beans. If you're starting with homemade ones, cook them longer first. You can eat the marinated beans alone or spoon them over salad or grilled meat or fish or mix them with grains.

Whisk the vinegar, garlic, mustard seeds, chile flakes, salt, and pepper in a large bowl. While whisking, drizzle in the oil and whisk until emulsified. Add the beans and fold until evenly coated. Transfer to a gallon-size resealable plastic bag and seal.

Place in a shallow dish just in case any liquid leaks. Refrigerate, turning the bag over occasionally, for at least 24 hours.

Make ahead: The beans can be refrigerated for up to 5 days.

Speedy Bacon and Three-Bean Skillet Stew

SERVES 6	*Everyday*

2 teaspoons canola oil

1 medium onion, finely chopped

1½ teaspoons kosher salt

4 ounces thick-cut bacon (about 6 slices), thinly sliced

1 garlic clove, sliced

1 Scotch bonnet or habanero chile, seeded and minced

3 (15-ounce) cans beans, preferably butter beans, small red beans, and pinto beans, rinsed and drained

1 (15-ounce) can low-sodium chicken broth

Bacon works a miracle here, making a twenty-minute stew of canned beans taste like it's been simmered from scratch all day long. Back in the day, cured pork and dried beans bubbled in cast-iron pots from sunrise to sunset. I get close to that with one little trick: I don't crisp the bacon. Listen, if we're talking breakfast bacon, I don't ever want to chew on a sad floppy strip. But stewed? Bacon should sizzle only until it's golden and just soft to maximize its flavor. At that point, its salty-sweet porky goodness soaks right into these creamy beans.

Want to make a good thing even better? Give the stew some garlicky zing with Serrano Kale Pistou (page 252) or scatter Hot 'n' Zesty Broccoli Panko Crunch (page 243) on top. Serve with Hot Water Cornbread (page 144) for dunking.

Heat the oil in a large deep skillet over medium-high heat. Add the onion and 1 teaspoon of the salt. Cook, stirring often, until just softened, 2 to 3 minutes. Push to one side of the pan, reduce the heat to medium-low, and scatter the bacon on the other side. Cook, stirring occasionally, until the fat renders and the bacon is golden but not crisp, about 5 minutes.

Add the garlic, chile, and the remaining ½ teaspoon salt. Cook, stirring, until the garlic is golden, about 1 minute. Add the beans and broth and bring to a simmer over medium-high heat. Reduce the heat to maintain a steady simmer and cook until heated through, about 5 minutes.

Make ahead: The beans can be refrigerated for up to 1 week. When you reheat them in the microwave or on the stove, stir in some water to loosen them up.

Field Peas ⎯WITH⎯ Country Ham

Everyday & *Celebration*

2 slices country ham, halved

1 onion, finely diced, plus more for serving

2 garlic cloves, chopped

2 tablespoons finely chopped fresh chile, such as Fresno

3 cups hulled fresh field peas

1 ripe tomato, cored, peeled, and diced

When I was a kid, my fingertips turned purple from the violet hulls of the pink-eyed peas I shelled for Granny. They're the light, fresh cousin to black-eyed peas. When you chew pink-eyed peas, they almost pop like a green pea, then end on a creamy note. But you can use this recipe for any field peas you can find. They're at any farm stand or supermarket in the summer throughout the South. In the rest of the country, seek them out at farmers' markets. They're the ideal side dish to whatever you throw onto the grill.

Put the ham, onion, garlic, and chile in a large saucepan and cover with 5½ cups cold water. Bring to a boil, then boil for 20 minutes.

Stir in the peas, return to a boil, then adjust the heat to maintain a steady simmer. Simmer until the peas are tender, about 30 minutes. Stir in the tomato and simmer until it starts to break down and thicken the broth, about 10 minutes.

Discard the ham (all its flavor has gone into the broth). The peas should be plenty salty from the ham, but you can taste and season with salt if you'd like. Divide the peas among serving bowls and top with fresh onion.

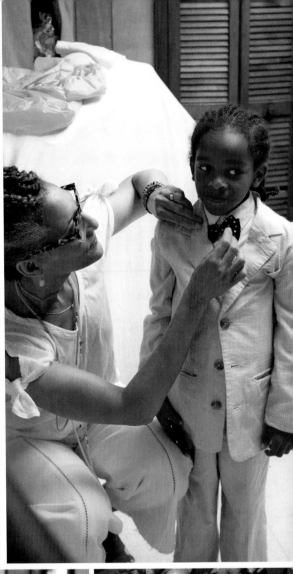

Happy 199th Year Mother Emmanuel

Saturday night in Charleston and I couldn't decide whether I wanted to go to Mother Emmanuel church the next morning. It wasn't because I stopped attending church years ago. It was because Mother Emmanuel, the oldest African Methodist Episcopal church in the South, was the site of a mass shooting by a white supremacist a year earlier. I didn't know if I wanted to see the site of such hate. Or if I wanted to go somewhere that had become symbolic of our nation's broken race relations.

Sunday morning and I figured we should go. My writer, Genevieve; photographer, Gabriele; and I were starting our journey through the South, and this felt like an important stop. As soon as we walked into the sanctuary, I was glad we went. That day, the parishioners were celebrating their 199th year as a church. Hearing the tumultuous history of the building and generations of leaders and congregants reminded me that this church is not defined by this one evil act. That it was not overcome by it. It had been through much more for a very long time. Through each phase of darkness, it emerged as light. With all that hate, it is a sanctuary of love and grace.

To commemorate their history, the choir sang, a dance troupe danced, and the lunch committee cooked a feast. Seeing those ladies at work in the kitchen reminded me of my own upbringing at John Calvin Presbyterian. Unspoken hierarchies ruled the stove. You had to work your way up to frying the chicken. If you dared bring potato salad, sister so-and-so's specialty, you would know to never commit that mistake again. And if you walk in as a chef who cooks on national television and distract the young women who want selfies with you, you better walk back out. I took one look at the head of the culinary committee and knew I was in trouble. She had a lot of food to finish before service let out. But I stayed a second longer. I just loved watching her stir a thick sauce of red beans into a big foil tray of rice, cutting chunks of butter into the mix.

Like so many women before her, she nourished Mother Emmanuel's congregants. Her food comforted them in the hard times, gave them more joy in the good times, and kept the community together in all times.

Pigeon Peas <u>AND</u> Red Rice

SERVES 8	*Everyday & Celebration*

1 (15-ounce) can pigeon peas, rinsed and drained

2 cups long-grain Carolina rice

3 tablespoons unsalted butter

1 onion, finely diced

Kosher salt and freshly ground black pepper

2 garlic cloves, finely chopped

1/2 teaspoon dried thyme

2 tablespoons tomato paste

4 cups unsalted vegetable broth

Donna, a fellow former caterer from Washington, D.C., and a dear dear friend, taught me this technique of mixing red sauce with beans and raw rice before baking them together. That way, you don't have to worry about the rice steaming properly and you save yourself a pot to wash. The oven's even heat cooks the grains just right while letting them absorb all that sauce. The only tricky thing with this dish is making sure you use a vegetable broth that doesn't have mushrooms or tomatoes, which make the liquid murky and turn the dish into an unappetizing khaki color. You want a golden stock for a pretty dish.

Preheat the oven to 350°F.

Mix the peas and rice in a 2½-quart shallow baking dish.

Melt the butter in a large saucepan over medium-low heat. Add the onion and ½ teaspoon salt and cook, stirring often, until translucent, about 5 minutes. Add the garlic, thyme, and ½ teaspoon pepper. Cook, stirring, for 1 minute. Add the tomato paste and cook, stirring, until the raw flavor cooks out, about 3 minutes.

Stir in the broth and bring to a boil over high heat. Once it's bubbling hard, pour it over the rice and pea mixture. Stir well, spread in an even layer, and cover with parchment paper and then foil.

Bake until the rice is just cooked through, about 35 minutes. Carefully uncover and serve hot.

Slow Cooker Baked Beans

SERVES 12	*Celebration*

Kosher salt and freshly ground black pepper

2 pounds dried great northern beans, or other small white beans, picked over, rinsed, and drained

1 tablespoon vegetable oil

2 medium onions, finely chopped

1 jalapeño chile, minced

2 garlic cloves, minced

1 tablespoon smoked paprika

1 teaspoon cayenne pepper

1 tablespoon Worcestershire sauce

¾ cup ketchup

⅓ cup packed dark brown sugar

¼ cup molasses

3 tablespoons yellow mustard

Baked beans take time. Something I'm short of. To get them evenly soft and full of flavor, I let them go in the slow cooker. All it takes is a little planning. I brine the beans in salt water overnight so they're tasty all the way through, then I throw them into the machine with my homemade sauce. They can hang out there on the warm setting after cooking too, so you can serve hot beans at your party without fuss. And these are some tasty beans! Slow cooking in my sauce gives them a porky richness even though this is meatless. But they'd taste great with any meat dishes or as the center of a vegetarian meal.

Stir 3 tablespoons salt into 3 quarts water until the salt dissolves. Add the beans, cover, and soak in the refrigerator until fully plumped, at least 6 hours and up to overnight.

Drain the beans and transfer to a 6-quart slow cooker.

Heat the oil in large saucepan over medium heat. Stir in the onions, jalapeño, and garlic and cook, stirring occasionally, until the onions are translucent, about 5 minutes. Add the smoked paprika, cayenne, 2 teaspoons salt, and 1 teaspoon black pepper. Cook, stirring, until the spices smell toasted, about 1 minute. Add the Worcestershire sauce, ketchup, brown sugar, molasses, and mustard. Cook, stirring, until the sugar dissolves and the mixture bubbles.

Pour the sauce into the slow cooker with the beans. Add enough water (about 5 cups) to cover by 2 inches.

Cover the cooker and cook on low until the beans are tender, 6 to 8 hours, stirring once or twice as they cook. Serve hot.

Make ahead: The beans can be refrigerated for up to 1 week. Reheat before serving.

Cornmeal

Johnnycakes

Celebration

1 cup fine yellow stone-ground cornmeal

1/2 cup all-purpose flour

1 tablespoon sugar

2 1/4 teaspoons baking powder

1/2 teaspoon salt

1 cup buttermilk

2 large eggs

1/4 cup vegetable oil, plus more for cooking

Exploring soul food led me to discover some Native American dishes too. Or, more accurately, showed me what came before us. As with our families and bloodlines, our culinary histories—one indigenous to this land, one brought over—are intertwined. Take these johnnycakes. I had assumed they were a soul food staple, but the most widely held history is that they came from the corn-growing Native Americans in what is now Rhode Island. Some say the name derived from the name of the tribe, Shawnee. Others think it's a mutation of "journey cake," because johnnycakes traveled well. Folks argue over exactly how a johnnycake should be prepared, too, but one commonality is that they're made with cornmeal and another is that they're flat and griddled like pancakes. Oh, and that they're delicious.

I tinkered for a year to perfect my formula. These golden corn cakes end up crisp around the edges and fluffy in the middle. They're a touch sweet, so you can douse them with syrup for breakfast or use them with savory fillings as sandwich bread (see page 66). Of course, I tear into them hot off the pan, but they hold up well and stay tasty at room temperature too.

Heat a griddle or large cast-iron skillet over medium heat.

Whisk the cornmeal, flour, sugar, baking powder, and salt in a large bowl. Whisk the buttermilk, eggs, and oil in a medium bowl until smooth. Pour the wet ingredients into the dry ingredients and gently fold until evenly moistened. You don't want lumps, but you don't want to overmix either.

Pour a thin sheen of oil onto the griddle or skillet. Drop a scant 1/4 cup batter onto the hot surface and spread into a 3-inch round. Working in batches if necessary, repeat with the remaining batter, spacing the rounds 1 inch apart. Cook until the undersides are golden brown and the tops are lightly bubbling, about 2 minutes. Flip carefully and cook until the other side is browned, about 1 minute longer. Transfer to a wire rack until ready to serve.

Hot Water Cornbread

Everyday

Hot water cornbread's one of those things you don't get unless you grew up with it. I'm here to help you get it. Because it's so good! First thing you should know: it's not bready or bread-like. These golden patties are more like tater tots, crunchy crust on the outside with an almost creamy center. Sprinkle enough salt on them and you'll be happy to munch on them plain. But their real purpose? To sop up all the saucy stuff from dinner—pot likker, meat juices, bean broths. Tear open a patty, hold the open end in the sauce, and it sucks the liquid right up, flavoring the cornmeal with the sauce and the sauce with the cornmeal.

I like to match my sprinkles to the dish I'm serving the cornbread with. If I'm putting it in a coconut-scented stew, I'm grating fresh lime zest on the patties. For something spicy? A pinch of cayenne. For something herbaceous? Minced parsley.

I'm not gonna lie: this cornbread is really easy *and* really hard to make. There are only a few ingredients and it takes fifteen minutes start to finish. But you gotta get each step right to nail that crunchy-creamy texture without it going all dense like a hockey puck. It took me years to match my granny's cornbread. Only after countless failures—even bastardizing Granny's original with wheat flour and eggs!—did I come up with this foolproof formula. The key? Cook the cornmeal enough to soften it but not stiffen it. It needs to go into boiling water, then it needs to get off the heat so that not too much water evaporates. And you need to start with fine *white* stone-ground meal, *not* yellow cornmeal or polenta. The fresher the better. Finally, fry the patties at a steady sizzle so they won't absorb too much oil but will develop a golden crust.

You can get it right the first time because I've gotten it wrong lots of times. Once you do, you'll be so happy to have this superfast side dish ready for any meal any night of the week.

1 cup fine white stone-ground cornmeal

$\frac{1}{2}$ teaspoon baking powder

2 tablespoons trans-fat-free vegetable shortening

$\frac{1}{2}$ teaspoon salt, plus more for sprinkling

Vegetable oil, for frying

Whisk the cornmeal and baking powder in a small bowl.

Combine the shortening, $\frac{1}{2}$ teaspoon salt, and $1\frac{1}{2}$ cups water in a medium saucepan and bring to a boil over medium heat, stirring to melt the shortening. Add the cornmeal mixture in a slow, thin stream, stirring steadily with a wooden spoon the whole time. When all of the cornmeal has been added, turn off the heat. Stir vigorously, scraping the bottom and edges of the saucepan, until the mixture is firm and slapping against the sides of the pan. The mixture should feel soft and not grainy. Let it cool until you can handle it with your hands.

Scoop $1\frac{1}{2}$ tablespoons dough, using a cookie scoop if you have one, into your hand and shape into a $\frac{1}{3}$-inch-thick patty. Repeat with the remaining dough.

Fill a large cast-iron skillet with oil to a depth of $\frac{1}{8}$ inch. Heat over medium heat until shimmering. Add enough patties to fit in a single layer with 1 inch between them. You may have to work in batches.

Fry, flipping once, until golden brown, 4 to 5 minutes per side. You don't want the oil too hot or the outsides will burn before the inside is hot, so adjust the heat if necessary. Drain on paper towels and immediately sprinkle with salt. Serve hot.

Skillet Cornbread

MAKES ONE 12-INCH BREAD; SERVES 12 | *Everyday* & *Celebration*

2½ cups fine white stone-
   ground cornmeal

1 tablespoon baking powder

1½ teaspoons salt

3 large eggs

1¾ cups buttermilk

2 tablespoons packed
   brown sugar

3 tablespoons rendered
   bacon fat or lard

I adored my godmother's cornbread. My godmother, Kitty Pulley, lived on Whites Creek Pike around the corner from our place on Haynes Meade Circle. I'd go over to play with her daughter Aurelia and she'd serve us wedges of cornbread hot from the pan. There was always this mysterious smoky sweetness to her bread, and I couldn't figure out what it was. But I loved it.

When I was creating this recipe, I started with lard, but ran out. There was some bacon fat in the fridge, so I used that instead. After a bite, I screamed, "Oh my God! It's Mrs. Pulley's cornbread! Bacon fat!!! It was bacon fat all along!" Like every good Southern cook, including my granny, Mrs. Pulley kept a crock of rendered bacon fat and stirred that secret ingredient into her cornbread. So go out and buy some good bacon. Pour the rendered fat through a sieve and keep that liquid gold in your fridge. It'll make this the tastiest cornbread you've ever had.

Preheat the oven to 425°F.

Whisk the cornmeal, baking powder, and salt in a large bowl. Whisk the eggs, buttermilk, and brown sugar in another bowl until smooth. Whisk the wet ingredients into the dry ingredients.

Heat the bacon fat in a 12-inch cast-iron skillet until liquid. Swirl it around to coat the bottom and sides of the skillet, then pour the rest into the batter. Whisk the batter until smooth, then pour into the hot skillet. Immediately transfer to the oven.

Bake until golden brown and a toothpick inserted in the center comes out clean, about 25 minutes. Serve warm.

Spoonbread Dressing

Celebration

4 tablespoons (2 ounces) unsalted butter, softened

1 onion, finely diced

1 celery stalk, finely diced

Kosher salt

1/2 teaspoon Poultry Seasoning (page 239) or store-bought salt-free poultry seasoning

2 cups whole milk

1 tablespoon sugar

1 cup fine yellow stone-ground cornmeal

1 (11-ounce) can sweet corn niblets, drained

1 teaspoon baking powder

3 large eggs

Oh. My. God. Did I just create the best Thanksgiving dressing ever? Why, yes, yes I did. You're welcome. I got all the flavors of classic dressing (that's stuffing to you Northerners)—onion, celery, sage—and suspended them in a creamy one-pan cornbread. With this recipe, I've saved you the step of baking a whole loaf of cornbread just to crumble into a side dish. Anything I can do to make your home cooking easier and tastier, I'll do. This just saved you a whole lotta time on Thanksgiving and it's gonna get you a whole lotta praise.

Preheat the oven to 350°F. Use 1 tablespoon of the butter to generously grease a shallow 3-quart casserole, Dutch oven, or baking dish.

Melt the remaining 3 tablespoons butter in a large pot over medium heat. Add the onion, celery, and 1 1/2 teaspoons salt. Cook, stirring occasionally, until translucent and just tender, about 4 minutes. Add the poultry seasoning and cook, stirring, for 1 minute.

Add the milk, sugar, and 1 cup water and bring to a boil. Continuously whisk the mixture while you pour in the cornmeal in a slow, steady stream. Keep whisking while the mixture bubbles rapidly until the cornmeal has absorbed all the liquid and is thick and smooth, about 5 minutes. Remove from the heat and stir in the corn and baking powder. Cool, stirring often, until lukewarm. Don't let the mixture clump.

Whisk the eggs in a large bowl until pale yellow and very foamy with no liquid remaining. Add one third of the beaten eggs to the cornmeal mixture and stir to loosen the cornmeal mixture. Add half of the remaining eggs and fold gently until incorporated, then repeat with the remaining eggs. Spread evenly in the prepared dish.

Bake until golden brown and set without any jiggling, about 25 minutes. When you press the top, it should spring back. Serve hot or warm.

Glorified Grits Soufflé

SERVES 12	*Celebration*

4 tablespoons (2 ounces) unsalted butter, plus more for the dish

2½ cups whole milk

3½ cups water

2 cups grits

2 teaspoons salt

1 cup grated cheddar cheese

4 large eggs, separated

Rise up! It's time to rise up, grits! This may be the ultimate soul food celebration. You take some everyday grits and give them a little milk, cheese, and eggs. Poof! They become this tower of fluffy creaminess. It's delicious as a side dish with just about anything and can be a showstopping vegetarian main dish too.

Preheat the oven to 425°F. Butter an 8-cup soufflé dish.

Combine the milk, water, grits, and salt in a large saucepan and bring to a boil over high heat, stirring occasionally. Reduce the heat to medium and continue boiling, stirring often, for 25 minutes. Add the butter and stir until melted. Reduce the heat to low and simmer, stirring occasionally, until the grits are soft, about 15 minutes more.

Remove from the heat and let cool for 5 minutes, stirring occasionally. Vigorously stir in the cheese and egg yolks. Let cool to lukewarm, stirring occasionally. The mixture needs to stay loose and not clump.

Whisk the egg whites in a large bowl until soft peaks form. Stir one-third of the beaten whites into the grits mixture to loosen it. Fold in half of the remaining whites until incorporated, then fold in the remaining whites until only a few white streaks are left. Pour the mixture into the prepared dish and smooth the top.

Bake until puffed and golden brown, about 45 minutes. Serve hot or warm.

Klaklo: Plantain Corn Pancakes

| *Celebration*

1 cup fine yellow stone-ground cornmeal

1 teaspoon baking powder

$1/8$ teaspoon cayenne pepper

$1/4$ teaspoon salt

$1/4$ teaspoon freshly ground black pepper

1 ripe plantain, peeled

2 large eggs

Vegetable oil, for frying

New York City cab rides are one of my favorite places to learn about new dishes. Sometimes asking drivers what they love most from their home countries is better than asking how they're doing. On one ride, a guy from Ghana replied, "Klaklo!" That was new to me, so I did some digging. Originally from Côte d'Ivoire, klaklo are fritters made with overripe plantains. To give them a Southern twist, I added cornmeal to my batter and panfried them flat like johnnycakes, so there would be more crisp outside to the almost creamy center. The ripe plantain—be sure to get a black one—gives these a little sweetness, so you can enjoy them for breakfast or as a side dish.

Whisk the cornmeal, baking powder, cayenne, salt, and black pepper in a small bowl.

Mash the plantain in a large bowl. Add the eggs and whisk until smooth. Add the cornmeal mixture and fold until you can't see the dry ingredients.

Fill a large cast-iron skillet with oil to a depth of $1/4$ inch and heat over medium heat until shimmering. Drop 2 tablespoons batter into the hot oil and spread into a $3^1/2$-inch round. Repeat, spacing the rounds 1 inch apart, until the skillet is full. Fry, flipping once, until both sides are browned, 3 to 4 minutes. Drain on paper towels. Repeat with the remaining batter, replenishing and reheating the oil as needed. Serve hot or warm.

Another thing about finding your HAPPY...if you don't know who YOU are, you can't find anything that will make you happy.

Breads

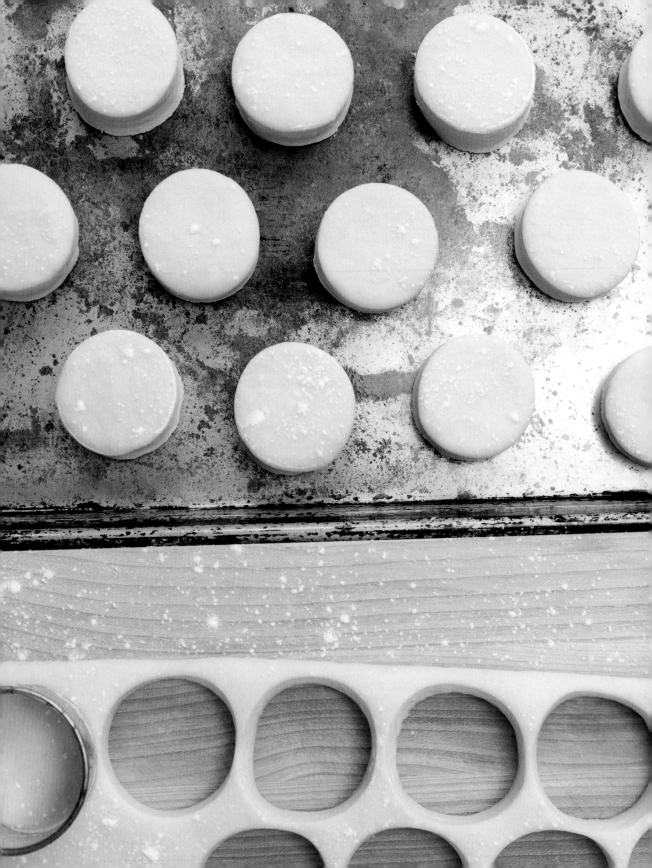

BISCUITS

Whenever I make biscuits by hand, I think of Granny. She had fingers as flat as spatulas, which was how she turned her dough quickly into light-as-air biscuits. Even though she never gave me a step-by-step tutorial in biscuit making, she showed me by example. She cut the butter evenly into the dry ingredients fast enough to keep it cold so that it could steam in the oven to create all those flaky layers. She knew to handle the dough gently at every step, since "roughness leads to toughness." When I started making biscuits on my own, I'd be shakin' in my boots, worried they'd come out heavy as hockey pucks. What I learned over the years is that it takes lots of practice to master the light hand needed for melt-in-your-mouth tender biscuits. You get a better feel for it with each batch.

So when I realized that I'd have cooks working in my restaurant kitchen without much—or any—biscuit experience, I had to figure out a way to ensure perfect biscuits even at the hands of novices. The trick? Grating frozen butter. You can use the large holes of a box grater or the lightning-speed shredder of a food processor. Both cut frozen butter into even bits fast, keeping the fat nice and cold. Even if you've never made biscuits before, you'll end up with perfect ones with this technique.

After that first step, you get to choose your own adventure. If you're short on time, do the tender, cakey drop biscuits (page 158). If you have loads of time, go for the yeasted roll-like angel biscuits (page 162), which need to rise. For anything in between, cut classic buttermilk biscuits (page 160) for flaky, buttery rounds.

Sorghum Drop Biscuits

8 tablespoons (4 ounces) unsalted butter, frozen, plus softened butter for the pan

2 cups all-purpose flour, plus more for the dough

½ cup sorghum flour

1 tablespoon baking powder

1 teaspoon sugar

1 teaspoon salt

½ teaspoon baking soda

2 tablespoons trans-fat-free vegetable shortening

1 cup cold buttermilk

Sorghum Butter (page 250), for serving

Down South, we make biscuits with White Lily flour. It produces feather-light biscuits because it's ground finer and sifted more than all-purpose flour. It's milled from soft red winter wheat, which has a lower protein content than regular flour, meaning it produces less gluten, which is what makes bread denser and chewier. To get the effect of White Lily with regular all-purpose, I mix in some sorghum flour, another traditional Southern ingredient. Ground from sorghum, which is actually in the grass family, the flour has no gluten at all. And thanks to the popularity of the gluten-free diet, you can find sorghum flour in supermarkets now. It has hints of malt in taste and makes these drop biscuits delicate and tender.

Preheat the oven to 450°F. Butter a large cast-iron skillet.

Mix both flours, the baking powder, sugar, salt, and baking soda in a large bowl with an open hand, using your fingers as a whisk. Add the shortening and use your fingertips to pinch it completely into the flour until the mixture resembles coarse crumbs.

Using a box grater, grate the frozen butter on the large holes into the flour. Toss until all of the pieces are coated. Add the buttermilk to the flour mixture. Using your hand as a spatula, gently mix until the dough forms a shaggy mass. Scrape the dough off your hand.

Using a large spoon or cookie scoop, drop 16 mounds of dough into the prepared skillet, spacing 1 inch apart.

Bake until golden brown, about 20 minutes. Serve warm with sorghum butter.

Make ahead: You can let the biscuits cool completely, then freeze them for up to 2 months. To serve, thaw them and then bake in a 350°F oven until toasted and warm.

Flaky Buttermilk Biscuits

8 tablespoons (4 ounces) unsalted butter, frozen, plus more; for the pan

2½ cups all-purpose flour, plus more for shaping the dough

1 tablespoon baking powder

1 teaspoon sugar

1 teaspoon salt

½ teaspoon baking soda

2 tablespoons trans-fat-free vegetable shortening

1½ cups cold buttermilk

I'm gonna come out and say it because you're gonna think it: these taste like Popeye's biscuits. (At least the back-in-the-day Popeye's.) Why, thank you. They do. These are what biscuits should be. They're flaky, with layers so fine they melt in your mouth. There's just enough flour and leavening to rise them up, so the fat doesn't weigh them down into greasy pucks. And there's plenty of buttermilk to keep them moist. That makes the dough sticky, so work fast and handle the dough as lightly as possible. Featherlight biscuits will be your reward.

Butter a half-sheet pan.

To make the dough with a food processor: Combine the flour, baking powder, sugar, salt, and baking soda in a food processor fitted with the blade attachment. Pulse a few times, until well mixed. Add the shortening and pulse until fine crumbs form. Switch to the grating disk attachment. With the machine running, push the frozen butter through the feed tube.

Transfer the mixture to a large bowl and toss to make sure all the butter shreds are coated with the floury crumbs. Add the buttermilk and fold in using a rubber spatula, running the flat of it through the center of the mixture and then around the edge while you rotate the bowl. Keep at it, being as gentle as possible, until the dry ingredients are evenly moistened.

To make the dough by hand: Mix the flour, baking powder, sugar, salt, and baking soda in a large bowl with an open hand, using your fingers as a whisk. Add the shortening and use your fingertips to pinch it completely into the flour until the mixture resembles coarse crumbs.

Using a box grater, grate the frozen butter on the large holes into the flour. Toss until all the pieces are coated. Add the buttermilk to the flour mixture. Using your hand as a spatula, gently mix until there are no dry bits of flour left. The dough will be sticky.

Lightly coat your work surface with nonstick cooking spray, then flour. (The spray keeps the flour in place.)

Turn the dough out onto the prepared surface and gently pat into a 1/2-inch-thick rectangle. Sprinkle the dough with flour, then fold it in thirds like a letter. Repeat the patting, sprinkling, and folding twice, rotating the dough 90 degrees each time. Pat the dough to 3/4-inch thickness. It should no longer be sticky.

Flour a 2-inch-round biscuit cutter and press it straight down into the dough. Transfer the round to the prepared pan, placing the bottom side up. Repeat, cutting the rounds as close together as possible and spacing them 1 inch apart on the pan. Stack the scraps, pat to 3/4-inch thickness, and cut again. Refrigerate the rounds until cold, at least 15 minutes.

Preheat the oven to 450°F.

Bake until the tops are golden brown and crisp, about 16 minutes. Let cool for 5 minutes on the pan before serving hot.

Make ahead: You can let the biscuits cool completely, then freeze them for up to 2 months. To serve, thaw them and then bake in a 350°F oven until toasted and warm.

Angel Biscuits

Everyday & Celebration

2 tablespoons active dry
    yeast

¼ cup warm water

¼ cup plus 1 teaspoon
    sugar

5 cups all-purpose flour,
    plus more for the dough

2 teaspoons baking powder

1 teaspoon baking soda

1 tablespoon salt

4 tablespoons trans-fat-free
    vegetable shortening

1 cup (8 ounces) unsalted
    butter, frozen

1 cup buttermilk

If you've ever been to Loveless Café in Nashville, I don't have to tell you what an angel biscuit is. For the rest of you, it's a cross between traditional short-dough biscuits and yeast-dough dinner rolls. Angel biscuits give you the best of both worlds. The tender biscuits have that irresistible yeasty aroma and tang *and* can be split and pulled apart in thin layers. They're perfect for mini sandwiches (see page 19) and they keep well too.

Mix the yeast, warm water, and 1 teaspoon of the sugar in a small bowl. Let stand until foamy, about 5 minutes.

Whisk the flour, baking powder, baking soda, salt, and the remaining ¼ cup sugar in a large bowl. Add the vegetable shortening and cut it in with your fingers until the mixture resembles coarse meal. Grate the butter on the large holes of a box grater. Add to the flour mixture and toss until evenly coated. Add the buttermilk and yeast mixture and fold until everything is evenly moistened. Knead gently with your hands in the bowl until the dough forms a ball. Cover tightly with plastic wrap and refrigerate for 2½ hours.

Turn the dough out onto a floured surface and flatten with your hands into a 1-inch-thick rectangle. Flour the top of the dough and roll into a 13 by 17-inch rectangle. Fold in the top and bottom thirds the way you'd fold a letter. Rotate the dough 90 degrees and roll into an 11 by 15-inch rectangle. Fold in thirds again, rotate, and roll to ½-inch thickness. The dough should be about 12 by 14 inches.

Using a floured 2-inch round cutter, cut the dough into rounds. Press straight down with the cutter and cut the rounds as close as possible. Lightly coat 2 baking sheets with nonstick cooking spray and place the rounds on each sheet, spacing them ½ inch apart. You can put the scraps on the sheets too or fry them to make doughnuts (see variations).

Loosely cover the dough rounds with plastic wrap and let rise while the oven heats to 350°F, about 30 minutes.

Bake until golden brown and baked through, 15 to 20 minutes. Serve hot or warm.

Rye Biscuits

Use 3^1/$_2$ cups all-purpose flour and 1^1/$_2$ cups light rye flour instead of all white flour. Sprinkle the tops with kosher salt and freshly ground black pepper before baking.

Cinnamon Sugar Doughnuts

Mix ^{1}/$_4$ cup sugar, ^{1}/$_2$ teaspoon ground cinnamon, ^{1}/$_4$ teaspoon ground ginger, and ^{1}/$_4$ teaspoon salt in a medium bowl. Cut the dough scraps into 1-inch pieces; it's okay for them to be irregular. Working in batches, fry them in 2 inches of vegetable oil that's been heated to 375°F. Fry until browned, 1 to 2 minutes. Drain on paper towels, then immediately toss in the sugar mixture to coat.

Make ahead: You can let the biscuits cool completely, then freeze them for up to 2 months. To serve, thaw them and then bake in a 350°F oven until toasted and warm.

The doughnuts are best eaten immediately.

Zucchini Cheddar Bread

Unsalted butter, for
    greasing

2 cups grated zucchini

1 cup whole wheat flour

1 cup all-purpose flour

1 teaspoon baking powder

3/4 teaspoon baking soda

1/2 teaspoon salt

1/4 teaspoon freshly ground
    black pepper

Pinch of cayenne pepper

1 1/2 cups grated cheddar
    cheese, plus more for
    sprinkling

2 tablespoons chopped
    scallion

2 large eggs

3/4 cup buttermilk

1/4 cup extra-virgin olive oil

Quiche meets bread in this savory quick loaf. Zucchini keeps the cheesy crumb nice and moist. You can top slices with eggs or sandwich cold cuts between them or enjoy them plain. If you pan-sear a slice in butter, the inside will get all custardy too. Yep, you want to try it.

Preheat the oven to 350°F. Butter a 9 by 5-inch loaf pan, line the bottom with parchment paper, and butter the parchment.

Gently squeeze the zucchini between paper towels to remove excess liquid. Whisk both flours, the baking powder, baking soda, salt, black pepper, and cayenne in a large bowl. Add the zucchini, cheese, and scallion and toss until evenly coated and separated.

Whisk the eggs, buttermilk, and oil in another large bowl until blended. It's okay if the liquid looks a little broken. Add the flour mixture and fold until evenly moistened. Pour into the prepared pan. Spread evenly and sprinkle a little cheese on top.

Bake until a tester inserted in the center comes out clean, about 50 minutes. Let cool in the pan on a wire rack for 10 minutes, then turn out of the pan and cool completely on the rack.

Make ahead: You can let the bread cool completely, then freeze for up to 2 months. To serve, thaw and then bake in a 350°F oven until toasted and warm.

Sweet Potato Rolls

MAKES 3 DOZEN	*Celebration*

1¼ cups whole milk

½ cup mashed sweet potato

2 tablespoons sugar

1 packet (2¼ teaspoons) active dry yeast

1 large egg, beaten, at room temperature

4 cups all-purpose flour

2 teaspoons salt

8 tablespoons (4 ounces) unsalted butter, cut into 1-inch pieces, at room temperature; plus 6 tablespoons (3 ounces), melted; plus more for your hands, softened

Vegetable oil, for the bowl

A little sweet potato kneaded into yeasted dough makes rolls extra soft and sweet. Down South, we like our bread so tender that it's sometimes on the edge of underbaked. I affectionately call those squishy rolls. These orange-tinted rounds can—and should—be baked all the way through. They'll end up as supple as any squishy ones.

In a small saucepan, combine the milk, sweet potato, and sugar and heat over medium heat, whisking to dissolve the sugar, until lukewarm (90 to 110°F). Remove from the heat and whisk in the yeast and egg. Let stand until foamy, about 5 minutes.

Beat the flour and salt in a stand mixer fitted with the paddle attachment on low speed until blended. Add the milk mixture in a steady stream. Mix until just moistened, about 1 minute. With the machine still on low, add the 8 tablespoons room-temperature butter, one piece at a time, beating until each piece is incorporated before adding the next and scraping down the sides and bottom of the bowl occasionally. It's okay if the dough looks broken at this point. Beat on medium speed until the dough is well combined and looks scrappy, about 2 minutes.

Swap the paddle for the dough hook attachment and knead the dough on medium-low speed until nice and smooth, about 5 minutes, occasionally scraping the dough off the hook and from the sides and bottom of the bowl. Transfer the dough to a very lightly oiled metal bowl. Turn the dough to coat in the oil, then cover loosely with plastic wrap. Let rise in a warm place until doubled in size, about 1 hour.

Uncover the dough and gently press down with your hands. The dough should be sticky without actually sticking to your fingers. Cover loosely with plastic wrap again and let rest for 5 minutes. Line 2 half-sheet pans with parchment paper.

Coat your hands with softened butter, as if you're washing your hands in the butter. Pinch off a golf ball–size piece of dough, then squeeze it through your thumb and index finger of one hand into a tight ball. The motion is similar to squirting water at someone in the swimming pool. You need a bigger opening between your fingers for dough than for water, but it's the same squirting-squeezing motion. Place the ball on the prepared pan, with the pinched side against the pan. Repeat with the remaining dough, spacing the balls of dough $1\frac{1}{2}$ inches apart. Cover the pans of dough lightly with plastic wrap. Let rise in a warm place until doubled in size, about 1 hour.

Preheat the oven to 400°F.

Uncover the rolls and brush the tops with the melted butter. Bake until light golden brown and cooked through, about 15 minutes. Serve hot or warm.

Make ahead: You can let the rolls cool completely, then freeze them for up to 2 months. To serve, thaw and then bake them in a 350°F oven until toasted and warm.

Benne Clover Leaf Rolls

1 cup whole milk

6 tablespoons sugar

4 1/2 teaspoons (2 packets) active dry yeast

4 tablespoons (2 ounces) unsalted butter, softened, plus more for the bowl and muffin pans

1 1/2 teaspoons salt

3 large eggs

4 cups all-purpose flour, plus more as needed

2 teaspoons benne (white sesame) seeds

Nothing smells better than baking rolls. Nothing. Especially when nutty benne seeds are toasting on top of them. If you've ever thought kneading dough would be fun but you haven't tried it, these rolls are for you. The springy soft dough pushes back with a satisfying tension with each push and turn and rolls easily into cute little balls. The process is foolproof and the result is bread so tender it tastes like a big hug.

Heat the milk and sugar in a small saucepan over medium-low heat until just warm to the touch. Pour into the bowl of a stand mixer, stir in the yeast, and let stand until foamy, about 5 minutes.

Add the butter, salt, 2 of the eggs, and 1 cup of the flour. Beat with the paddle attachment on low speed until smooth. With the machine running, add the remaining flour 1/2 cup at a time, scraping the bowl occasionally. As soon as all the flour is incorporated, switch to the dough hook.

Knead with the dough hook on low speed, scraping the bowl and hook occasionally, until the dough is smooth and elastic, about 10 minutes. It will be sticky.

Generously butter a large bowl and flour a work surface. Turn the dough out onto the surface and knead into a tight ball. Transfer to the bowl and turn the dough to butter the whole ball. Cover the bowl with plastic wrap and let stand until doubled in size, about 1 1/2 hours.

Generously butter two 12-cup muffin pans. Punch down the dough and turn out onto a work surface. Use a bench scraper or sharp knife to cut the dough into six even 1-inch-wide strips. Cut each strip into twelve 1-inch pieces. Roll a piece into a ball and tug and pinch the edges of the dough under the ball to form a tight, seamless round. Place in a muffin cup. Repeat with 2 more pieces and tuck into the same cup. Repeat with all the dough, putting a trio of balls into each cup. Cover loosely with plastic wrap and let stand until the dough puffs just above the rim, about 20 minutes.

Preheat the oven to 375°F.

Beat the remaining egg with 1 tablespoon water in a small bowl until smooth. Brush the tops of the dough balls very gently with the egg wash. Try not to deflate the dough! Sprinkle the tops with the benne seeds.

Bake until golden brown and baked through, 10 to 15 minutes. Serve warm.

Make ahead: You can let the rolls cool completely, then freeze them for up to 2 months. To serve, thaw them and bake in a 350°F oven until toasted and warm.

Poultry

HOT CHICKEN

My life can be measured in fried chicken. Ten years old and munching on Grandma Thelma's perfect version for my uncle's Broadway debut in *Bubbling Brown Sugar*. Sixteen and burnin' up my mouth at Prince's Hot Chicken, hangin' out late with high school friends. Twenties and rejecting it 'cause I was learning fancy French cuisine in cooking school. Thirties and cooking it on my own for the first time, making my catering clients at Radio One and neighborhood barbershops so happy. Forties and shying away again, not wanting to be pigeonholed as a soul food cook in professional circles. Fifties and embracing my heritage by opening a hot chicken restaurant. All along, it was a constant: church lunches, Sunday suppers, reunions.

Fried chicken's so special, let's keep it that way. It's a celebration food. Even when I owned a fried chicken joint, I told customers they couldn't have it every day. Collards, slaw, green beans, yams, peas? Have all the sides you want! But save the chicken as a treat. That's what our farming ancestors did. They couldn't eat chicken more than a few times a year. If they did, they'd lose their source of eggs. As we came up in the world, migrated north, and had the option of fried chicken all the time, we shifted from our vegetable-centric diet. I'm sure I would've too. When you finally get to have what you've been deprived of for so long, of course you're gonna indulge. But that's taken a toll I don't need to tell you about. We all know.

So when you have something to celebrate, whip out this recipe. And give friends and family the food love they deserve. Splurge on organic young birds. Be careful with the cooking. It's easy for the skin to brown too much under the weight of the bird before the meat's cooked through. I attend to the bubbling chicken pieces as though they're my kids, watching like a hawk and asking, "How you doin', baby?" (What? You don't talk to your food?) I turn and angle the pieces so they'll brown evenly, turning the heat up and down to keep the temperature steady.

Pineapple-Habanero Honey Fried Chicken

SERVES 10	*Celebration*

2 whole chickens
(3 pounds each)

2 tablespoons onion
powder

2 tablespoons garlic
powder

2 tablespoons plus 2
teaspoons sweet paprika

2 tablespoons cayenne
pepper

Kosher salt

1/4 cup dill pickle juice
(from a jar of pickles)

2 cups all-purpose flour

Vegetable oil, for frying

Pineapple Habanero Hot
Sauce (page 246)

Honey, for serving

My seasoning mix packs enough spice to make the chicken super tasty on its own. But if you want more sweet and heat, give the chicken a splash of hot sauce and a ribbon of honey.

Cut each of the chickens into 10 pieces: 2 drumsticks; 2 thighs; 2 wings; and 2 breasts, each cut in half. Put in a gallon-size resealable plastic bag.

Mix the onion powder, garlic powder, 2 tablespoons of the paprika, 1 tablespoon of the cayenne, and 2 tablespoons salt in a small bowl. Sprinkle half of the mixture over the chicken in the bag, then shake the bag and massage the spices into the meat evenly. Pour the pickle juice over and massage again. Let stand at room temperature for 15 minutes.

Meanwhile, mix the flour with the remaining 2 teaspoons paprika, 1 tablespoon cayenne, and 1 tablespoon salt in another gallon-size resealable plastic bag. Transfer the chicken to the flour mixture. Shake the bag and toss the chicken around, pressing the flour mixture against it, until every piece is well coated. Transfer the coated pieces to a half-sheet pan.

Fill a large cast-iron skillet with oil to a depth of 1/2 inch. Heat over medium heat until a pinch of flour sizzles the second it hits it (340°F).

Fry the chicken in batches. Add a few pieces to the hot oil, skin side down. Fry, turning the pieces to evenly brown and adjusting the heat to maintain 340°F, until the meat is cooked through, 10 to 15 minutes, depending on the size of the piece. Drain on paper towels.

Transfer to a serving platter and drizzle with hot sauce and honey. Serve hot.

Make ahead: The marinated chicken (before the flour is added) can be refrigerated for up to 4 hours.

Barbecued Chicken Legs

Celebration

1 recipe Barbecue Spice
Blend (page 240)

¼ cup distilled white
vinegar

2 pounds chicken
drumsticks (about 5)

2 pounds chicken legs
(about 2)

1 cup Barbecue Sauce
(page 245)

Every summer cookout in Nashville had to have barbecued chicken legs. I loved the way barbecue sauce charred onto the meat and ended up all over my fingers. My sauce does exactly that, caramelizing on the chicken skin. To make sure the meat has plenty of flavor, I marinate it in a spice and vinegar blend. The acid helps the seasonings get all into the meat in the time it takes the grill to heat.

Mix the barbecue spice and vinegar in a large bowl. Add the chicken and turn until evenly coated. Let stand while you prepare the grill.

Heat a charcoal grill with the coals banked to one side. When the coals are ashed over and hot, carefully grease the grill grate.

Put the chicken over the hot coals skin side down and grill, flipping once, until browned and seared, about 5 minutes. Transfer to the side of the grill with no coals, skin side up.

Cover the grill with the vents open and let the chicken cook over indirect heat until cooked through, about 35 minutes.

Uncover the grill and move the chicken back over the coals. Brush with the barbecue sauce and grill, flipping and brushing, until the sauce is caramelized onto the meat, about 5 minutes. Serve hot.

Make ahead: The marinated chicken can be refrigerated for up to 4 hours before grilling. The cooked chicken can be refrigerated for up to 3 days.

Molasses Baked Chicken Wings

SERVES 6	*Celebration*

3 pounds chicken wings

Kosher salt and freshly ground black pepper

1/2 cup molasses

1/2 cup packed light brown sugar

1/3 cup fresh orange juice

1/4 cup cider vinegar

2 garlic cloves, grated on a Microplane

1 teaspoon grated peeled fresh ginger

1 teaspoon cayenne pepper

Finger-lickin' wings mean party time! I wanted to show off the funky sweetness of molasses, which is cane syrup that's been boiled down. It has a long history as a staple sweetener in African-American cooking. Here, I've cooked it even further with orange juice and vinegar to create a sticky sweet-and-sour glaze for wings. Ginger and cayenne give them an easy little kick.

Preheat the oven to 450°F. Line a half-sheet pan with parchment paper and fit a wire rack into the pan.

Season the chicken with 1 teaspoon salt and 1 teaspoon black pepper. Arrange in a single layer on the prepared rack. Roast until the skin is taut and the meat is par-cooked, about 30 minutes.

Meanwhile, combine the molasses, brown sugar, orange juice, vinegar, garlic, ginger, cayenne, and 1 teaspoon salt in a small saucepan and bring to a boil, stirring to dissolve the sugar. Reduce the heat to maintain a simmer and simmer until syrupy, about 15 minutes.

Transfer the wings from the rack to the parchment. Pour the syrup over them and toss to coat evenly. Arrange the wings in a single layer.

Roast, flipping the wings and spooning syrup over them every 10 minutes, until glazed and caramelized, about 30 minutes.

Use tongs to carefully transfer the wings to a serving platter, leaving the sauce in the pan behind. Serve when they're cool enough to handle.

Make ahead: The cooked wings can be refrigerated for up to 3 days.

Baked Chicken ⊞ Pan Gravy

| **SERVES 6** | *Everyday & Celebration* |

2 teaspoons onion powder

2 teaspoons garlic powder

2 teaspoons sweet paprika

1 teaspoon cayenne pepper

6 chicken legs, excess fat trimmed

Kosher salt

2 onions, very thinly sliced

6 garlic cloves, lightly smashed and peeled

1/4 cup unsalted chicken stock

We rolled up to Sugar's Place in the middle of the day in the middle of July. Across the street from the Mississippi College School of Law in Jackson, this little restaurant has some of the best soul food I've ever eaten. I walked in with no appetite and left wishing I had eaten more. And I couldn't stop thinking about its baked chicken. Chef-owner mother-son team Glenda Cage Barner and Donovan Barner worked some magic with those chicken legs. The meat pulled right off the bone but still had a nice chew. You could taste the seasonings all the way through the meat. Onions melted into the jus shimmering around the chicken. It felt as warming as a beloved family meal but like the fantasy version—where your family makes the best chicken in the world.

I'm not going to claim this chicken is as good as Glenda's. You've got to get yourself to Jackson to judge. But I think I've come pretty close. Generously spiced, these chicken legs hang out in the oven for a while, so they're perfect for company. All you have to do before serving is smash the garlic and onion to make a light pan sauce to spoon all over the fork-tender meat.

Preheat the oven to 350°F.

Mix the onion powder, garlic powder, paprika, and cayenne in a small bowl. Season the chicken generously with salt, then sprinkle with the spice mixture. If you have time, cover and refrigerate for at least 4 hours and up to overnight.

Toss the onions and garlic in a 3-quart shallow glass or ceramic baking dish. Spread in an even layer and put the chicken skin side up on top. Pour the stock all around. Cover the dish tightly with foil.

Bake until the chicken is cooked through, about 1 hour. Uncover the dish and flip the chicken in the pan juices. Arrange the pieces skin side up again. Bake uncovered until the meat is fork tender and the skin is lightly browned, about 30 minutes longer.

Transfer the chicken to a serving platter. Use a fork to smash the garlic and onions into the pan juices and stir well to form a light pan gravy. Season to taste with salt and spoon all over the chicken.

Make ahead: The spice-rubbed chicken can be refrigerated overnight. The cooked chicken can be refrigerated for up to 3 days.

Piri Piri Poultry

SERVES 4 TO 6	*Everyday* & *Celebration*

Roasted Piri Piri Poussins or Cornish Game Hens

4 (1-pound) poussins or Cornish game hens, spatchcocked

1 recipe Piri Piri Spice (page 241)

Kosher salt

Extra-virgin olive oil

Once I discovered through my DNA testing that I have Portuguese ancestry, I decided to claim it as my personal terroir in the kitchen. And then I realized that DNA wasn't the only thing traveling around with the Portuguese colonizers. One iconic dish—piri piri chicken—has deep African roots. This is my take on the spicy grilled chicken.

Piri piri is a type of chile that originated in the Americas and was taken to Africa by the Portuguese in the sixteenth century. Though it probably arrived in West Africa, it made its way south and east on the continent and became especially popular in Mozambique and Angola. In fact, "piri piri" means "pepper pepper" in Swahili. The hot peppers spice chicken throughout the southern countries of Africa and in Portugal.

There are countless combinations of piri piri chiles and chicken, each unique to the region and cook. In the case of my version, a hot spice rub marinates the bird before a nice turn over a grill's fire or a long run in the oven. You can make it with either baby chickens or big ones, according to the instructions below.

Heat a charcoal grill with the coals banked to one side. When the coals are ashed over and hot, carefully grease the grill grate.

Sprinkle the poussins all over with the spice mixture and lightly season with salt. Drizzle with oil and gently rub the oil all over to coat.

Put the poussins over the hot coals skin side down and grill until browned and seared, about 3 minutes. Transfer to the side of the grill with no coals, skin side up.

Cover the grill with the vents open and let the poussins cook over the indirect heat until cooked through, about 30 minutes.

Transfer to a serving platter and let rest for at least 5 minutes before serving.

Roasted Piri Piri Chicken

One (3-pound) chicken

1 recipe Piri Piri Spice
(page 241)

Kosher salt

Extra-virgin olive oil

Preheat the oven to 425°F. Fit a rack into a half-sheet pan.

Sprinkle the chicken inside and out with the spice mixture and lightly season with salt. Drizzle with oil and gently rub the oil all over to coat. Truss the chicken and place on the prepared pan.

Roast until browned and the juices run clear, about 50 minutes.

Transfer to a serving platter and let rest for at least 10 minutes before carving.

Make ahead: The spice-rubbed chicken can be refrigerated for up to overnight. The cooked chicken can be refrigerated for up to 3 days.

Brown Sugar Baked Chicken

| SERVES 4 | *Everyday & Celebration* |

1/4 cup packed brown sugar

1/2 teaspoon ground coriander

1/4 teaspoon cayenne pepper

Zest and juice of 1 lime

2 tablespoons vegetable oil

Kosher salt

3 pounds bone-in, skin-on chicken legs or thighs

The weekend I saw *Bubbling Brown Sugar*, the musical showcasing music from the Harlem Renaissance, changed my life. I watched it with my family in New York City, where we shared a feast of the best chicken I had ever had. I was just a kid from Nashville then, but I knew. I wanted to be on stage. And I wanted more chicken. I'm so thankful I got to fulfill both dreams. This is my way of honoring that memory. Brown sugar bubbles as a tangy hot glaze for lip-smackin' chicken.

Preheat the oven to 375°F.

Mix the brown sugar, coriander, cayenne, lime zest and juice, oil, and 1 teaspoon salt in a large bowl. Add the chicken and toss until evenly coated. Arrange skin side down in a single layer in a 9 by 13-inch glass or ceramic baking dish. Sprinkle lightly with salt.

Bake for 30 minutes. Flip the chicken to evenly coat with the pan juices and arrange skin side up in a single layer. Return to the oven and bake until the skin is browned and the meat is cooked through, about 30 minutes more.

Transfer the chicken to a serving platter. Skim the fat off the pan juices and discard or put the juices through a fat separator. Pour the skimmed juices all over the chicken and serve.

Make ahead: The cooked chicken can be refrigerated for up to 3 days.

Caribbean Smothered Chicken WITH Coconut, Lime, and Chiles

SERVES 4	*Everyday* & *Celebration*

1 teaspoon vegetable oil

4 large bone-in, skin-on chicken thighs (1½ pounds)

Kosher salt and freshly ground black pepper

6 large sprigs thyme

2 large onions, thinly sliced

2 garlic cloves, chopped

1 habanero chile, slit

1 cup light coconut milk

Zest and juice of 1 large lime, plus wedges for serving

½ teaspoon Curry Powder (page 242) or store-bought mild yellow curry powder

Smothered pork chops may be an iconic soul food specialty, but this recipe proves you can smother anything. All it really means is coating slow-cooked meat with a blanket of saucy aromatics that end up as gravy too. Here, I've buried chicken thighs under a Caribbean-inspired coconut milk simmer of onions, garlic, and, of course, chile. Finally, the curry powder and lime balance the richness with spiced heat and a bright citrus pop.

Heat the oil in a shallow Dutch oven or casserole with a lid over high heat. Season the chicken generously with salt and pepper and add to the hot oil, skin side down. Sear, flipping once, until browned on both sides and the fat renders, about 5 minutes.

Push the chicken to one side of the pan, add the thyme and onions to the other side, and reduce the heat to medium-low. Cook, stirring, until the onions get some color, about 4 minutes. Add the garlic, chile, ½ teaspoon salt, and ½ teaspoon pepper. Cook, stirring, for 1 minute, then add the coconut milk and ¼ cup water. Bring to a boil, stirring.

Arrange the chicken in a single layer skin side up and surround with the onion mixture. The skin should be just above the liquid line. Cover and simmer until the chicken is cooked through, about 20 minutes.

Uncover and stir in the lime juice. Simmer uncovered until the sauce thickens, about 5 minutes. Stir in the curry powder and lime zest. Serve immediately with lime wedges.

Make ahead: The cooked chicken can be refrigerated for up to 3 days.

Chicken Meatloaf Balls

Everyday & Celebration

$^1/_2$ cup quick-cooking oats

$^1/_4$ cup whole milk

1 large egg

2 tablespoons grated onion

1 garlic clove, grated on a
   Microplane

1 tablespoon finely chopped
   fresh parsley leaves

1 pound ground chicken

$^1/_2$ teaspoon dried thyme

$^1/_4$ teaspoon cayenne
   pepper

1 tablespoon vegetable oil,
   plus more for frying

Kosher salt and freshly
   ground black pepper

This thirty-minute dish is for Mama. Tender and comforting with classic meatloaf herbs, these meatballs develop a caramelized crust from skillet cooking. They taste like the meatloaf she made for me when I was a kid. Mama's food may not win any awards, but she created this safe space where she; my sister, Kim; and I ate and shared our lives. Mama's the glue that holds our family together. I hope I can pick up that baton. Starting with these meatloaf balls. The truth is, Mama's a picky eater. And she doesn't want to spend too much time in the kitchen. Whenever I ask her what she wants, she says, "You know me, Carla. I just want a little piece of chicken." Well, here you go, Mama. I hope you love it as much as I love your meatloaf.

Mix the oats and milk in a large bowl. Let stand until the oats absorb the milk, about 5 minutes. Add the egg, onion, garlic, and parsley and mix well. Add the chicken, thyme, cayenne, 1 tablespoon oil, $^1/_2$ teaspoon salt, and $^1/_4$ teaspoon black pepper. Mix with your hands until everything is evenly distributed.

Heat $^1/_8$ inch oil in a large skillet over medium heat. Using a $1^1/_2$-tablespoon cookie scoop, scoop the meat mixture and drop it into the skillet. You can use a measuring tablespoon too—scoop a heaping mound, then use your finger to push it into the skillet. Scoop and drop the remaining meat, spacing the balls apart.

Fry, turning and flipping to evenly brown, until cooked through, 12 to 15 minutes. Serve hot.

Make ahead: The meatloaf ball mixture can be refrigerated for up to overnight before shaping and frying. The cooked meatballs can be refrigerated for up to 3 days.

Brunswick Stew

8 bone-in, skin-on chicken thighs

1 tablespoon vegetable oil

Kosher salt and freshly ground black pepper

1 large onion, diced

2 carrots, diced

2 celery stalks, diced

3 garlic cloves, sliced

$\frac{1}{2}$ teaspoon dried thyme

$\frac{1}{4}$ teaspoon chile flakes

2 tablespoons tomato paste

1 (14.5-ounce) can diced tomatoes

4 cups unsalted chicken broth

1 bay leaf

1 pound Yukon gold potatoes, scrubbed and cut into $\frac{1}{2}$-inch pieces

2 cups frozen lima beans

$1\frac{1}{2}$ cups fresh corn kernels

1 cup sliced okra

$\frac{1}{3}$ cup Worcestershire sauce

$2\frac{1}{2}$ tablespoons apple cider vinegar

3 tablespoons light brown sugar

My great-aunt Lucille's husband made the best Brunswick stew. She goes on and on about the garden vegetables in his pot—lima beans, string beans, cabbage, whatever's coming up in abundance. Those vegetables helped stretch what little chicken or pork they had on the farm in this catchall dish. But it didn't taste like deprivation. It tasted of bounty. When I was creating this dish, I channeled Lucille's spirit in her telling of Brunswick stew, which I hadn't had growing up. I collected all that looked good at the market and really let it stew. Going against my French culinary training and going with my culinary heritage, I simmered the vegetables and chicken all together for a whole hour. Each vegetable remained intact and tasted fresh even as they all united into a delicious whole. I promise you, this most comforting stew is one to remember.

Toss the chicken with the oil and 1 teaspoon salt in a large bowl. Heat a large Dutch oven over medium-high heat. Sear the chicken in batches, flipping once, until golden brown, about 5 minutes. Transfer to a plate. Pour out almost all the fat from the oven.

Reduce the heat to medium. Add the onion, carrots, celery, and $\frac{1}{2}$ teaspoon each of salt and pepper. Cook, stirring, for 3 minutes. Add the garlic, thyme, and chile flakes and stir for 1 minute. Add the tomato paste and stir for 1 minute. Add the tomatoes, broth, and bay leaf; bring to a boil.

Stir in the potatoes, lima beans, corn, okra, and chicken. Bring to a boil, then reduce the heat to simmer 20 minutes.

Stir in the Worcestershire sauce, vinegar, brown sugar, and 1 teaspoon salt. Simmer until the chicken is tender, about 40 minutes. Discard the skin and bones of the chicken and tear the meat into large pieces. Return to the stew and serve hot.

Make ahead: The stew can be refrigerated for up to 3 days.

Dirty Rice

1 tablespoon vegetable oil

1 pound ground turkey

Kosher salt and freshly
ground black pepper

1 chicken liver, finely
chopped

1 chicken heart, finely
chopped

1 chicken gizzard, finely
chopped

1 onion, finely diced

1 celery stalk, finely diced;
plus more, very thinly
sliced, for serving

1 green bell pepper, finely
diced

1 garlic clove, chopped

1 sprig thyme

1¼ cups long-grain
Carolina rice

2½ cups unsalted chicken
broth

1 chicken neck

Hot sauce, for serving

When Mama and I dropped my sister, Kim, off in New Orleans for college, we played tourist too. I left with a stack of recipe cards, including one for dirty rice. I hadn't had it or heard of it and wondered why anyone would want to eat something "dirty." Now I'm grown and I know exactly why. That dirty is delicious! Chicken liver and gizzards, along with the trinity of onion, celery, and green bell pepper, turn white rice brown in this Cajun dish. And it all gives the rice a savory depth like the best parts of roast chicken. This rice is so rich, I like to top it with crunchy celery slices and sharp hot sauce.

Dirty rice reminds us that chickens are whole animals that come with all these parts most people would rather ignore. It's time for us to get back to the origins of the food we eat—and to eat every part without wasting. Get yourself a whole chicken and cut it up to enjoy both light and dark meat, then take the innards and neck for this rice. You can use the back and wing tips and any other parts to make the stock too, if you want.

Heat the oil in a large Dutch oven over high heat. Add the turkey, ½ teaspoon salt, and ½ teaspoon black pepper and press in a single layer. Sear until browned, about 2 minutes, then stir and break into small bits to brown, about 2 minutes longer. Add the chicken liver, heart, and gizzard and cook, stirring, until browned, about 1 minute.

Add the onion, diced celery, bell pepper, garlic, 1 teaspoon salt, and ½ teaspoon black pepper. Cook, stirring, until translucent, about 5 minutes. Add the thyme and rice and cook, stirring, until the rice is toasted, about 1 minute. Add a bit of the stock and scrape up the browned bits from the bottom of the Dutch oven. Once you've gotten them all, add the rest of the stock and the chicken neck and bring to a boil.

Cover, reduce the heat to low, and simmer for 17 minutes. Uncover, stir well, and cover again. Remove from the heat and let stand for 5 minutes. Serve with hot sauce and thinly sliced celery.

Make ahead: The dirty rice can be refrigerated for up to 1 day.

CHEFS are used to failure. We're trying out recipes and having to do them over and over again until they turn out right. If you're not failing, you're not trying.

Meat

Hot Dogs!

Hottugs. That's what my husband, Matthew, and I call 'em. Matthew's a vegetarian now and I don't eat much meat, but I love me a good hottug. It just better be worth it. Here's how to make 'em great:

- Buy good ones. Snappy skin, no mystery ingredients.

- Hot, then low. Give them a turn on the hot side of the grill to get nice grill marks, then let 'em roll over low heat. If you keep them on the hot side, the skin will burn and burst before the inside's hot. All those precious juices will go to the coals.

- When they're ready, they're ready. Once the inside's nice and hot, the dog will look and feel taut. If the dogs keep hanging out on the grill, they'll dry out and end up wrinkly and chewy. Yuck.

- Fresh buns. I like potato rolls and I buy them the day I'm eating them. I cradle the bag like a baby all the way from the store home. No one wants a smushed bun. Some folks will argue for toasted buns. You do you. But if the bread's fresh, I want a squishy roll around my snappy dog.

- Load 'em up. Ketchup and mustard? Check. Then throw down some homemade condiments for the best hot dogs ever. I'm talking chow chow (page 254), corn relish (page 260), red onion pickles (page 255), and Comeback Sauce (page 247).

- Eat! Gotta enjoy it while it's hot.

Ham Steaks with Cantaloupe and Blackberry Sauté

SERVES 4	*Everyday & Celebration*

1 tablespoon vegetable oil

4 small ham steaks, whole; or 2 large ham steaks, halved

1 small red onion, diced

Kosher salt

2 tablespoons sorghum or maple syrup

2 tablespoons fresh lemon juice

2 cups blackberries

2 cups cantaloupe cubes

When I got a whiff of ripe melon at the Charleston farmers' market, I had to stop and sniff it hard. I inhaled that heady honeyed scent and couldn't stop thinking about what I'd do with such a sugary cantaloupe. The only thing that could stand up to it would be salty ham. Turns out, it makes a great topper, along with saucy blackberries.

Heat the oil in a large skillet over high heat. Add the ham and cook, flipping once, until lightly browned and heated through, about 4 minutes. Transfer to serving plates.

Reduce the heat to low and add the onion and 1/2 teaspoon salt. Cook, stirring often, until the onion is lightly browned but not soft, about 3 minutes. Add the sorghum, lemon juice, and 1/4 cup water. Stir, scraping up any browned bits, until the mixture is reduced slightly, about 2 minutes.

Add 1 cup of the berries and cook, gently stirring occasionally, until the liquid in the pan has almost completely evaporated. Spoon the mixture over the ham, then scatter the cantaloupe and remaining berries on top. Serve immediately.

Clove ⚏ Cider Glazed Holiday Ham

SERVES 20	*Celebration*

One 6¹/₂-pound spiral-cut ham

1 cup fresh apple cider

¹/₄ cup packed dark brown sugar

2 tablespoons bourbon

2 tablespoons Dijon mustard

2 tablespoons unsalted butter

1 tablespoon apple cider vinegar

1 cinnamon stick

6 whole cloves

1 teaspoon freshly grated nutmeg

1 teaspoon whole black peppercorns

My homemade glaze brings the flavors from classic Southern curing with the smoky depth of bourbon, the complex saltiness of mustard, and the earthy sweetness of apple cider. The mixture thoroughly bakes into the ham, keeping it moist and tender, making this a totally foolproof centerpiece if you're cooking a feast for the first time.

Preheat the oven to 375°F.

Place the ham, cut side down, in a 9 by 13-inch glass or ceramic baking dish.

Place the remaining ingredients in a small saucepan. Bring to a boil over medium-high heat, whisking to blend in the sugar and mustard. Reduce the heat to maintain a steady boil and cook, whisking occasionally, until syrupy and reduced to ¹/₂ cup.

Pour the hot glaze with all the spices all over the ham. Bake, basting every 10 minutes, until the ham is heated through and well glazed, 35 to 40 minutes.

Transfer the ham to a serving platter. Strain the pan sauces through a sieve into a serving vessel. Serve the pan sauce with the ham.

Make ahead: Leftover ham can be refrigerated for up to a week. Stuff cold slices into sandwiches, chop them up for omelets, simmer into soup. The possibilities are endless!

HAM

Can I be honest here? I mean *really* honest? I didn't like country ham as a kid. I know, right? Yes, I'm a Southern girl. Yes, I love pork. But country ham was too intense for my young palate. It smelled like it was dug out of a fire pit, tasted so much like a living thing, even in its dry state. I love it now—for that very intensity and its funky funk, savory depth, smokiness, and chew that come with months of traditional curing, smoking, and aging.

Aging has improved me too—it gave me a proper appreciation for the curing process my ancestors created and upheld. With age comes the craving for the flavors of age. Beneath the mold-spotted skin on a well-aged ham, a crystalline saltiness is balanced by a nutty sweetness.

Country ham isn't meant to be carved and eaten in fat slabs—never was. It should be shaved into slices so thin the sun should be able to shine through. A shard can be sandwiched between biscuits (pages 158 to 162) or tossed into any vegetable dish to add a wham-bam hit of smoky saltiness. A ham was originally meant to last a family a whole year, until the following year's batch came out of the smokehouse.

As much as I adore country ham, I also love the juiciness of the ham we now commonly have for the holidays. It comes from the same part of the pig's hind leg, but is simply boiled before packaging. To make matters even easier, it can be bought presliced. It's city ham. For us city folks. Whichever ham you choose, be sure to save the bone to boil with greens or beans.

Bahamian Souse Soup ⊞ᵂᴵᵀᴴ Pork Belly ᴬᴺᴰ Potatoes

SERVES 8	*Everyday*

Zest of 1 lime

1 teaspoon apple cider vinegar

½ teaspoon cayenne pepper

2¼ teaspoons ground allspice

1 teaspoon dried thyme

3 tablespoons vegetable oil

Kosher salt

1½ pounds skinless pork belly, cut into 1-inch chunks

1 onion, diced

1 carrot, diced

1 celery stalk, diced

2 garlic cloves, sliced

2 jalapeño chiles, seeded and minced

1 bay leaf

1 red potato, scrubbed and diced

¼ cup fresh lime juice

Throughout the Caribbean, souse is a way to use up meat scraps. Pigs' feet, head, ears, and knuckles are cooked, then marinated in lime juice. Well, we're eating high on the hog now, aren't we? And I can't think of a better cut than pork belly. That tasty fat melts right into the tender meat while cooking. I've turned souse into a stew here, loading it up with vegetables and keeping that signature lime juice flavor by stirring in a generous dose right before serving. The result is a steaming hearty bowl of goodness that still tastes bright and feels light.

Mix the lime zest, vinegar, cayenne, 1 teaspoon of the allspice, ½ teaspoon of the thyme, 2 tablespoons of the oil, and 1 teaspoon salt in a large bowl. Add the pork and toss until evenly coated. Cover the bowl and refrigerate for 30 minutes.

Heat the remaining 1 tablespoon oil in a large Dutch oven or saucepan over medium-high heat. Add enough pork to fit in a single layer without crowding the pan. Cook, turning occasionally, until browned on all sides, about 7 minutes. Transfer to a plate. Repeat with the remaining pork.

Add the onion, carrot, and celery to the hot fat in the saucepan. Cook, stirring, for 1 minute. Add the garlic and jalapeños and cook, stirring, for 2 minutes. Add 1 teaspoon of the remaining allspice and the remaining ½ teaspoon thyme and cook, stirring, until the vegetables are browned but still crunchy, about 2 minutes. Add just enough water to scrape up the browned bits from the pan.

Add the bay leaf, pork and accumulated juices, 3 cups water, and 1 teaspoon salt. Bring to a boil, then reduce the heat to keep a simmer going. Simmer until the pork is tender, about 1 hour.

Add the potato and simmer until the potato is tender, about 20 minutes. Stir in the lime juice, the remaining $1/4$ teaspoon allspice, and $1/2$ teaspoon salt. Discard the bay leaf and serve hot.

Make ahead: The souse can be refrigerated for up to 3 days or frozen for up to 2 months.

Garlicky Grilled Pork Tenderloin
WITH Black-Eyed Pea Vinaigrette

Black-Eyed Pea Vinaigrette

1 garlic clove, grated on a
Microplane

1 scallion, thinly sliced

1 teaspoon Dijon mustard

1 teaspoon honey

1/2 teaspoon chile flakes

1/4 teaspoon cayenne
pepper

1/4 cup red wine vinegar

Kosher salt and freshly
ground black pepper

1/2 cup plus 2 tablespoons
extra-virgin olive oil

2 tablespoons torn fresh
parsley, plus more for
garnish

1 (15-ounce) can black-eyed
peas, rinsed and drained

1 small tart crisp apple,
cored and diced

Pork and beans: happiest marriage ever. I've taken this perfect food couple and lightened it into a weeknight dish. Tenderloin gets even juicier after a garlicky marinade and a turn on the grill. It's topped with crunchy apple and creamy black-eyed peas mingled in a refreshing vinaigrette.

To make the vinaigrette: Whisk the garlic, scallion, mustard, honey, chile flakes, cayenne, vinegar, and 1/2 teaspoon salt in a large bowl. While whisking, add the oil in a slow, steady stream. Fold in the parsley, peas, and apple. Season with salt and black pepper. Cover and refrigerate until ready to serve, at least 1 hour.

To make the pork: Cut the pork into eight 1/2-inch-thick slices at an angle. Using a meat tenderizer or rolling pin, gently pound the pork into flat, even slices about 1/3 inch thick. Whisk the oil, garlic, apple, scallion, mustard, honey, 1 teaspoon salt, and 1/4 teaspoon black pepper in a small bowl. Pour into a gallon-size resealable plastic bag and add the pork. Seal the bag and turn and massage the pork to work the marinade evenly into the meat. Refrigerate for at least 1 hour and up to 4 hours.

Heat a grill or grill pan over high heat. Bring the vinaigrette to room temperature.

Remove the pork from the marinade and lightly season with salt and black pepper. Grill the pork, turning once, until grill marks appear and the center is rosy pink, 6 to 8 minutes. Transfer to a serving platter and let rest for 5 minutes.

Pork Tenderloin

1 whole pork tenderloin
(1¼ pounds), silver skin
trimmed

2 tablespoons extra-virgin
olive oil

2 garlic cloves, minced

2 tablespoons grated apple

1 scallion, finely chopped

1 teaspoon Dijon mustard

1 teaspoon honey

Kosher salt and freshly
ground black pepper

Stir the black-eyed pea vinaigrette and spoon all over the pork. Garnish with parsley and serve immediately.

Make ahead: The vinaigrette can be refrigerated for up to overnight. The marinated pork can be refrigerated for up to 4 hours before grilling.

Slow Cooker Pulled Pork

Celebration

Barbecue Spice Blend
(page 240)

1 (5- to 6-pound) boneless
pork shoulder or butt
roast

Kosher salt and freshly
ground black pepper

1/2 cup ketchup

1/2 cup apple cider vinegar

1/2 cup distilled white
vinegar

1/3 cup light brown sugar

1/2 teaspoon chile flakes

1 bay leaf

2 garlic cloves, smashed

1 onion, quartered

Barbecue Sauce (page 245)

Nope, this isn't true pulled pork. That happens in a smoker, with at least fourteen hours of TLC. But this is an easy way to feed a crowd. Feeding folks is one of the most important things any of us can do. So I want to give this option to make it doable for anyone.

One family's been feeding pulled pork to hungry customers for more than seventy years on the same block in East Selma, Alabama. In the historically black neighborhood, Lannie's Bar-B-Q does a mean plate of its signature smoked pork, topped with a shard of crackling. That crisp pig skin's one of the best things I ever ate. And my conversation with Lula Hatcher, the current owner and granddaughter of founder Lannie Moore Travis, is one of the most memorable.

She welcomed me into her home across the street from her sturdy brick restaurant, where the next generation of the family now cooks. Sunk into her living room chair, she recalls, "It wasn't like it is now. When we first opened, we were the only place all could come. Everyone—black and white—came in through the *front* door."

Lula remembers the winter of 1965, when voting rights activists crowded into Lannie's to celebrate the news that Dr. Martin Luther King Jr. would come to town. She remembers that spring, when her dear friend Annie Lee Cooper was knocked down hard by Sheriff Jim Clark during protests downtown. She remembers the day of the march. The strength and grace in the face of violence. In the years before and after, Lula and her family kept smoking whole hogs and bringing plates and sandwiches to all the civil rights leaders and activists. They played their part by fueling the movement with food, delivering comfort and joy.

And they're still doing it today.

Sprinkle the spice blend all over the pork in a large bowl. Season the pork generously with salt and pepper. Cover and refrigerate for at least 4 hours and up to overnight.

Mix the ketchup, both vinegars, brown sugar, chile flakes, bay leaf, garlic, onion, and 1 teaspoon pepper in a 6-quart slow cooker. Add the pork, cover, and cook on low until fork-tender, 8 to 10 hours.

Carefully transfer the pork to a serving dish. Shred the meat with two forks. Strain the cooking liquid through a sieve. Skim off and discard the fat. Pour enough of the cooking liquid over the meat to moisten it. Serve hot, with the barbecue sauce.

Curried Lamb Stew ⚌ Potatoes

SERVES 8

Everyday

2 pounds bone-in lamb
    shoulder chops, meat
    cut into 1-inch chunks,
    bones reserved

2 tablespoons extra-virgin
    olive oil

Kosher salt and freshly
    ground black pepper

2 medium onions, cut into
    1/2-inch chunks

2 carrots, cut into 1-inch
    chunks

2 celery stalks, cut into
    1-inch pieces

5 garlic cloves, sliced

1 serrano chile, sliced

2 tablespoons tomato paste

2 cups unsalted chicken
    broth

1 cup canned diced
    tomatoes with their
    juices

1 pound red potatoes,
    scrubbed and cut into
    1-inch chunks

2 tablespoons Curry
    Powder (page 242) or
    store-bought yellow
    curry powder

1/4 teaspoon cayenne
    pepper

Everywhere I go, I ask folks, especially those far from home, what they love to eat most. It's my way of getting to really know people. So that's what I did when I met David, the farmer at Foot Print Farms in Jackson, Mississippi. He's from Jamaica, which explains why he didn't seem fazed by the oppressive midday summer heat. I, on the other hand, was hot as all get-out. While he was tossing bruised tomatoes to the goats snuffling around the field, he casually replied, "My favorite dish? Goat curry." Inspired by his descriptions of Jamaican curry, hot with chiles and sweet with tomatoes, I created this one. You can swap in goat for the lamb if you can find it. The Caribbean accents in this stew make it especially delicious when spooned over Cassava with Coconut Milk and Lime (page 110).

Preheat the oven to 325°F.

Toss the lamb and bones with 1 tablespoon of the oil and 1 teaspoon salt. Heat a large Dutch oven over medium-high heat. Working in batches, add the lamb and bones in a single layer, spacing them apart, and sear, turning and flipping to evenly brown, about 5 minutes. Transfer to a plate.

Reduce the heat to medium and add the remaining 1 tablespoon oil along with the onions, carrots, celery, garlic, chile, and 1/2 teaspoon salt. Cook, stirring often, for 3 minutes. Add the tomato paste and cook, stirring, for 1 minute. Add the chicken broth, tomatoes, potatoes, and lamb and bones with any accumulated juices. Bring to a boil, then cover and transfer to the oven.

Bake until the meat and vegetables are very tender, about 1 1/2 hours. Uncover and stir in the curry powder, cayenne, and 1/2 teaspoon salt. Season with black pepper and more salt. Serve hot.

Meaty Tomato Mac AND Cheese

Celebration

8 ounces macaroni

1 pound ground beef chuck

Kosher salt and freshly ground black pepper

1/2 cup finely chopped onion

2 garlic cloves, chopped

3 tablespoons tomato paste

1 teaspoon mustard powder

1/2 teaspoon paprika

1/4 teaspoon cayenne pepper

2 tablespoons unsalted butter

2 tablespoons all-purpose flour

2 cups whole milk

8 ounces sharp cheddar cheese, grated

What do you get when you cross mac and cheese with meaty tomato sauce? This pot of yum! Macaroni's curves catch all the melty cheddar beefiness of the sauce. This one-pot dish is super comforting on chilly days.

Cook the macaroni according to the package directions until al dente. Drain, rinse under cold water until cool, and drain again.

Meanwhile, heat a large Dutch oven over high heat until smoking hot. Add the beef, 1 teaspoon salt, and 1/4 teaspoon black pepper and spread in a single layer, breaking the meat into small bits. Cook until the bottom is nicely browned, about 5 minutes. Stir well, then push the beef to one side of the Dutch oven. Add the onion, garlic, 1/2 teaspoon salt, and 1/4 teaspoon black pepper to the other side. Cook, stirring occasionally, until the onion is translucent, about 3 minutes. Stir the onion mixture into the beef and push to one side of the Dutch oven again. Add the tomato paste to the other side, reduce the heat to medium, and stir for 1 minute. Stir into the beef until well mixed. Add the mustard powder, paprika, and cayenne and stir for 1 minute.

Reduce the heat to medium-low. Push everything to one side of the pot. Add the butter to the other side. When it melts, dump the flour over the butter. Stir the flour and butter until the raw flour cooks out, about 2 minutes. Stir the roux into the meat mixture.

While stirring, add the milk 1/4 cup at a time. Keep stirring until the mixture bubbles steadily for 2 minutes. Reduce the heat to low and stir in the cheese until melted.

Add the pasta and fold until evenly coated and hot. Season with salt and pepper and serve immediately.

OUR FAMILY RESTAURANT

Swett's is our home away from home. It's a Nashville institution, a meat-and-three cafeteria where you roll down the line with your tray, pointing to what you want. I always built my plate around a slab of meatloaf, loading up on greens and peas. That and the warm cornbread and hot candied yams and chilled chess pie.

Mama and Daddy went to Pearl High School with David Swett, the second-generation owner. They hung out there together in high school and they still do now, decades after they've divorced. It's where we all gather—my sister, Kim; my half brother, Daniel, with his wife and daughters; and Aunt Jackie.

David pushes tables together for our clan. Mama moves all the chairs. Technically, Mama's a customer, but really, she's the mayor of Swett's. While we get our food and sit down and eat, she makes the rounds, asking after babies and parents.

"Back in my time, we were a real community. We looked after each other." Like the nurse she is, Mama's still checking on everyone, making sure all is right.

Daddy, in the meantime, has me in stitches. He's a cool daddy-o. Loose and funny and lovable. Whenever we see each other, we crack each other up. His sister Jackie sits sweetly by. Kim chats with Daniel's girls, asking them about school and books like the teacher she is. Daniel and his wife find a moment to enjoy a meal without worrying about the kids a seat away.

Mama doesn't stop moving. Swett's really feels like home to her, so she's putting away leftovers, wiping up crumbs. That makes us all feel at home too.

Meatloaf ══ with ══ Spicy Ketchup

SERVES 8	*Everyday & Celebration*

Spicy Ketchup

³/₄ cup ketchup

2 teaspoons bottled horseradish

1 teaspoon ground cumin

¹/₂ teaspoon Worcestershire sauce

Pinch of cayenne pepper

Meatloaf

¹/₂ cup quick-cooking oats

¹/₄ cup milk

1 large egg, beaten

2 teaspoons ground cumin

¹/₂ teaspoon dried thyme

¹/₄ teaspoon cayenne pepper

2 garlic cloves, minced

¹/₄ cup fresh flat-leaf parsley leaves, very finely chopped

1 small onion, very finely chopped

1 celery stalk, very finely chopped

1 carrot, very finely chopped

2 pounds ground beef chuck

1 tablespoon Worcestershire sauce

Kosher salt and freshly ground black pepper

Mama didn't really cook. Didn't like it, didn't do it much. But meatloaf was her jam. Every once in a while, my sister, Kim, and I would get that special dinner, all slathered in ketchup. Honestly, I had forgotten about it until I had a meatloaf sandwich at a restaurant. After one bite, I started tearing up. It tasted just like Mama's meatloaf! My heart was flooded. Somewhere between being on her feet all day as a nurse and driving me and Kim to school and dance and theater, Mama made time to do what she liked least. For us. If that isn't cooking with love, I don't know what is.

In homage to Mama's version, I've kept mine all beef. But I couldn't resist spicing up the meat with veggies, cumin, and thyme. And plain ol' ketchup tastes so much better with the heat of horseradish and cayenne.

To make the ketchup: Stir the ketchup, horseradish, cumin, Worcestershire sauce, and cayenne until well mixed. Let stand while you prepare the meatloaf.

To make the meatloaf: Preheat the oven to 425°F. Line a half-sheet pan with parchment paper.

Mix the oats, milk, egg, cumin, thyme, and cayenne in a large bowl. Let stand for 5 minutes.

Add the garlic, parsley, onion, celery, carrot, beef, Worcestershire sauce, 2 teaspoons salt, and 1 teaspoon pepper to the bowl with the oats. Mix with your hands until everything is evenly distributed through the meat. Transfer to the prepared pan and pat into a 12 by 4-inch loaf.

Bake for 15 minutes. Brush with a thin layer of the spicy ketchup. Bake for 10 minutes, then brush again, more generously this time.

Reduce the oven temperature to 375°F. Bake until the top is lightly caramelized and a meat thermometer inserted in the center registers 150°F, about 40 minutes. Let stand for 5 minutes, then slice and serve with the remaining ketchup on the side.

Ghanaian Peanut Beef and Tomato Stew

Everyday & Celebration

1³/₄ pounds beef chuck, cut into 1-inch cubes

Kosher salt and freshly ground black pepper

2 tablespoons peanut or vegetable oil

1¹/₂ cups chopped onion

1 red bell pepper, seeded and cut into 1-inch chunks

¹/₂ habanero chile, seeded and finely chopped

2 garlic cloves, minced

2 tablespoons grated peeled fresh ginger

1 tablespoon ground cumin

2 carrots, cut into 1¹/₂-inch chunks

2 yams, peeled, quartered, and cut into 1-inch chunks

1 (14.5-ounce) can diced tomatoes

3 tablespoons creamy peanut butter

Chopped roasted peanuts, for serving

Lime wedges, for serving

Groundnut stew's popularity extends beyond Ghana throughout West Africa. Freshly roasted groundnuts (aka peanuts), which are naturally a little savory and sweet, thicken this hearty onion, pepper, and tomato mix. That vegetable trio forms the base of most West African stews. What goes in after that is up to the cook. I add meat to the mix to turn this into a really hearty one-pot meal. It's important to treat the meat right. First, you want to invest salt in the meat, coating it generously even before it hits the pot. Then, you need to brown it. Yep, it takes time, but if you don't do it, you'll end up with gray beef that tastes steamy. Finally, you have to let it simmer until it buckles under a butter knife. If you're gonna splurge on beef, you gotta do right by it. When you do, it's a delicious addition to this iconic stew.

Toss the beef with 2 teaspoons salt in a large bowl. Heat 1 tablespoon of the oil in a large Dutch oven over high heat. Add enough beef to fit in a single layer, spacing the cubes ¹/₂ inch apart. Cook, flipping and turning, until browned on all sides, about 7 minutes. Transfer to a plate. Repeat with the remaining beef.

Reduce the heat to medium and add the remaining 1 tablespoon oil, then the onion, bell pepper, and 1 teaspoon salt. Cook, stirring often, until the onion is just translucent, about 3 minutes. Add the chile, garlic, ginger, and cumin and cook, stirring, until fragrant, about 1 minute. Stir in the carrots, yams, tomatoes, beef with any accumulated juices, and 4 cups water. The liquid should cover the solids. If not, add more. Bring to a boil over high heat, then reduce the heat to medium-low, cover, and simmer until the beef is tender, about 1 hour and 20 minutes.

Ladle ¹/₂ cup cooking liquid into a small bowl. Add the peanut butter and ¹/₂ teaspoon black pepper. Stir until smooth. Pour the mixture back into the stew, along with ¹/₂ teaspoon salt. Stir well. Season to taste with salt and black pepper.

Divide among serving bowls, top with chopped peanuts, and serve with lime wedges.

Oxtail Stew ⚏ Brown Sauce

1/2 cup all-purpose flour

1/4 teaspoon paprika

1/8 teaspoon cayenne pepper

Kosher salt and freshly ground black pepper

6 large oxtails (2 1/2 pounds)

2 tablespoons vegetable oil

2 onions, halved and very thinly sliced

2 celery stalks, thinly sliced

4 garlic cloves, thinly sliced

1 tablespoon tomato paste

3 cups unsalted beef stock

2 teaspoons Worcestershire sauce

Dilled Cucumber and Celery Salad (page 71), for serving

The smell of meaty oxtails simmering in an oniony brown sauce takes me right back to Granny's Sunday suppers. *Mmm. So good!* This meat is tender enough to tug off with a fork, but not so soft that it's mush. And that gravy! All the flavor's in the brown. Most folks don't take the time to brown meat anymore, and that's a shame. You've got to do it here because that's how you end up with a deep, rich sauce. Just enjoy those minutes, turning the tails, telling some tales. That's what Sunday suppers are all about.

Preheat the oven to 325°F. Mix the flour, paprika, cayenne, 1/4 teaspoon salt, and 1/4 teaspoon black pepper in a shallow dish. Sprinkle the oxtails with 2 teaspoons salt, then roll them in the flour mixture to coat evenly. Shake off any excess flour.

Heat the oil in a large Dutch oven over medium-high heat. Add the oxtails and sear, turning and flipping to brown evenly, about 10 minutes. Transfer to a plate.

Add the onions and celery to the Dutch oven and reduce the heat to medium. Cook, stirring, until just softened, about 4 minutes. Add the garlic and 1 teaspoon salt and cook, stirring occasionally, until the vegetables are tender, about 4 minutes. Add the tomato paste and cook, stirring, until it loses its raw flavor, about 1 minute.

Add the stock and bring to a boil, stirring and scraping up any browned bits. Add the Worcestershire sauce and the oxtails with any accumulated juices. The liquid should come up to the shoulder of the meat, about three-quarters up the sides. If it doesn't, add some water.

Cover the Dutch oven with its lid and transfer to the oven. Bake for 1 hour and 40 minutes. Carefully uncover the pot and turn the oxtails over. Loosely tent with foil. Bake until the oxtails are fork tender and the juices are thickened, 30 to 45 minutes. Transfer the oxtails to a serving dish. Top with the dilled cucumber and celery salad and serve immediately with all the pan juices.

Seafood

Fried Fish <u>WITH</u> Spaghetti

Everyday & *Celebration*

Tangy Tomato Sauce
  (page 251)

12 ounces spaghetti

1 cup fine yellow cornmeal

½ cup all-purpose flour

1 teaspoon baking powder

½ teaspoon garlic powder

½ teaspoon dry mustard

¼ teaspoon cayenne
  pepper

Kosher salt and freshly
  ground black pepper

Vegetable oil, for frying

1 pound thin flaky white
  fish fillets, such as
  catfish, whiting, or
  flounder

You've never heard of fried fish with spaghetti? Well, then, you're not from Mississippi, Alabama, or Tennessee. It's a thing. A really good thing. Twirl tender noodles soaked with the rounded tartness of tomato sauce, then spear a piece of spicy crisp fish. You get hot, sour, sweet, heat, crunch, and chew all in one bite.

I forgot about this dish until chef Enrika Williams reminded me of it. After cooking professionally in Atlanta, New York, and Houston, Enrika returned home to her big family in Westpoint in northeast Mississippi. It's the kind of place where the town is so small and the extended families are so big that first dates start with a rundown of cousins to make sure the daters aren't related. It's also the kind of place where kids will check on Mrs. Jenkins down the street to make sure she's recovering from her illness and where any loss is followed by an icebox filled with neighbors' casseroles. It's where Enrika grew up on fried fish with spaghetti. As she remembers, "That dish was not up for negotiation."

Neither were the pinto beans slow cooked with smoked jowls, nor was the coconut cake with extra frosting for birthdays or the crystal punch bowl for Grandma's card parties. Enrika grew up cooking with her mom and grandma and visiting her grandfather's farm and chickens. "This is where my ideas and imagination started. I got it in the red clay dirt of Mississippi." And this dish, more than any other, captures home for her.

Heat the tomato sauce in a large saucepan until simmering. Keep warm. Cook the spaghetti according to the package directions.

Meanwhile, mix the cornmeal, flour, baking powder, garlic powder, dry mustard, cayenne, 1 teaspoon salt, and ¼ teaspoon black pepper in a large shallow dish.

Fill a large cast-iron skillet with oil to a depth of ½ inch and heat over medium-high heat until hot. A pinch of the cornmeal should sizzle when it hits the oil. Dredge a fish fillet in the cornmeal until evenly coated, shake off the excess, and carefully lay it in the hot oil. Repeat with another fillet or two—however many you can get in there to fit comfortably without crowding.

Fry, carefully flipping once, until golden brown, 2 to 3 minutes per side. Transfer to a wire rack to drain, and let cool. Repeat with the remaining fish, replenishing and reheating the oil between batches.

Drain the spaghetti and toss with the tomato sauce until evenly coated. Divide among serving plates, along with the fish. Serve hot.

Grilled Salmon with Mustard Sauce

SERVES 4	*Everyday*

¼ cup yellow mustard

2 tablespoons apple cider vinegar

2 teaspoons light brown sugar

¼ teaspoon cayenne pepper

½ teaspoon Worcestershire sauce

2 tablespoons vegetable oil, plus more for the salmon

4 thick center-cut skin-on salmon fillets (about 6 ounces each)

Kosher salt and freshly ground black pepper

Anytime I get fried fish in the South, I squirt tangy yellow mustard, not Dijon, all over it. I love that kick with fish. Since I save fried foods for special occasions, I came up with this mustard sauce to enjoy over grilled salmon for daily meals. It's also delicious on grilled chicken or pork.

Whisk the mustard, vinegar, brown sugar, cayenne, Worcestershire sauce, and 2 tablespoons oil in a small bowl. Let stand while you prepare the salmon.

Heat a grill, preferably a charcoal one, to high heat.

Generously rub the salmon all over with oil, then season generously with salt and black pepper. Put on the hot grill grate skin side down. Cover the grill and cook until a cake tester or thin-bladed knife slides easily through the salmon, about 12 minutes. It should be a paler shade on the outside but still slick in the center for medium-rare.

Slide a fish spatula under the salmon to transfer to serving plates. The fish should come right off. If the skin sticks to the grate, then slide the spatula between the flesh and skin to get the fish off the grill in one beautiful piece.

Drizzle the mustard sauce all over the salmon and serve.

Salmon Patties

1 pound thick skinless
salmon fillet

Kosher salt and freshly
ground black pepper

2 tablespoons grated onion

2 tablespoons mayonnaise

2 tablespoons plain
breadcrumbs

1 teaspoon Dijon mustard

Vegetable oil, for cooking

Salmon patties and I go way back. When I spent the night at my grand-mother Thelma's house, I'd wake up to salmon patties sizzling on the grid-dle. She'd set them in grits for a big plate breakfast. My dad made the same recipe for dinner when Kim and I stayed with him. He seasoned canned fish with salt and pepper, bound the rounds with breadcrumbs, and fried them up. When I cooked salmon patties in professional kitchens, I made them with fancy herbs and spices. Now, I'm going back to the simple seasonings of my childhood with fresh salmon. The trio of onion, mayonnaise, and mustard is all good salmon needs.

If you have leftover cooked salmon, skip the first step for an even quicker meal. You'll need 2 cups flaked salmon. The patties are delicious over grits (see page 230). They're also tasty with salad or other vegetables.

Preheat the oven to 400°F. Line a small rimmed baking sheet with foil.

Sprinkle the salmon all over with salt and pepper and put on the prepared baking sheet. Bake until the white protein is just starting to come out of the fish, about 15 minutes.

When the salmon is cool enough to handle, transfer to a large bowl and flake the flesh. You should have 2 cups. Add the onion, mayonnaise, bread-crumbs, and mustard. Gently fold until well mixed, then season with salt and pepper. Shape into six 1-inch-thick patties ($2\frac{1}{2}$ inches in diameter).

Heat a thin layer of oil in a large nonstick skillet over medium-high heat. Add the patties and cook, flipping once, until browned, about 2 minutes per side. Cover and cook until heated through, about 2 minutes longer. Serve hot.

Roasted Whole Chile-Stuffed Fish

SERVES 4

Everyday & Celebration

2 whole striped bass
(1¼ pounds each),
gutted and scaled

Kosher salt

1 red habanero chile

1 lemon

1 lime

1 cup fresh flat-leaf parsley
leaves

1 tablespoon fresh thyme
leaves

1½ teaspoons allspice
berries, coarsely ground

5 tablespoons extra-virgin
olive oil

1½ teaspoons grated peeled
fresh ginger

A citrus-chile blend—fresh with herbs, warm with allspice, hot with ginger—gets roasted in fish, then spooned all over it. That one-two punch of Bahamas-inspired seasonings makes this dish so delicious. If you're intimidated by cooking whole fish, don't be. It's easier to handle than fillets. Because the meat's on the bone, it can't dry out, and because the skin's still on, it won't stick to the pan. Just choose fish with bright eyes, firm flawless flesh, and red gills. Be sure to ask the folks at the fish counter to gut and scale the fish for you; that's some messy business. It's okay if you can't get striped bass. Any whole fish with mild white flesh, like branzino or red snapper, works too. Just increase the cooking time if the fish are bigger.

Preheat the oven to 450°F. Line a half-sheet pan with foil.

Cut 4 slits on each side of each fish and place on the pan. Salt the fish cavities. Cut 2 sides off the habanero chile and put 1 piece in each fish cavity. Discard the stem and seeds from the chile and mince the remaining sides. Remove 2 strips of zest each from the lemon and lime using a vegetable peeler and put 1 strip of each in each fish cavity. Reserve the fruit.

Mix ½ cup of the parsley, 1½ teaspoons of the thyme, ½ teaspoon of the allspice, 1 teaspoon of the habanero, 1 tablespoon of the oil, and ½ teaspoon salt in a bowl. Divide between the fish cavities. Rub the remaining 4 tablespoons oil all over the fish; season with salt.

Roast until the fish is opaque and tender, about 25 minutes.

Meanwhile, very finely chop the remaining ½ cup parsley and 1½ teaspoons thyme. Mix with the ginger, remaining habanero, 1 teaspoon allspice, and ¼ teaspoon salt in a bowl. Zest in the remaining lemon and lime, then squeeze in 2 teaspoons juice from each fruit.

Transfer the fish to a platter. Pour the oil out of the pan into the herb mixture. Stir, then spoon all over the hot fish.

Braised Plantains WITH Shrimp

3 teaspoons vegetable oil

3 very large ripe plantains
(2$\frac{1}{2}$ pounds total),
peeled, halved
lengthwise, and cut into
1-inch slices crosswise

1 onion, finely chopped

Kosher salt and freshly
ground black pepper

2 garlic cloves, finely
chopped

$\frac{1}{2}$ teaspoon cayenne
pepper

1 (14.5-ounce) can whole
peeled tomatoes

1 teaspoon grated peeled
fresh ginger

1 habanero chile, slit open

1 bay leaf

12 ounces shell-on shrimp

Hot sauce, for serving

Plantains may look like bananas, but they're much starchier and much lower in sugar. Native to the Caribbean, they're cooked every which way, depending on their ripeness. When they're yellow with some black speckles, they're ideal for braising. They're starchy enough to hold their shape, but a little sweet too. Here, I've stewed them with a Caribbean-inspired blend of tomatoes, ginger, and chile. Topping the braise with shrimp turns this into a hearty one-dish meal.

Heat 1 teaspoon of the oil in a large, deep cast-iron or nonstick skillet over high heat. Add half of the plantains in a single layer without crowding and sear, flipping once, until browned and no longer sticking to the skillet, about 5 minutes. Transfer to a plate. Repeat with another 1 teaspoon oil and the remaining plantains.

Add the remaining 1 teaspoon oil to the pan and reduce the heat to medium. Add the onion and $\frac{1}{2}$ teaspoon salt. Cook, stirring, for 2 minutes. Add the garlic, cayenne, and $\frac{1}{4}$ teaspoon black pepper. Cook, stirring, for 1 minute. Crush the tomatoes with your hands and add to the skillet, along with any juices from the can and a can of water. Stir in the ginger, habanero, bay leaf, $\frac{1}{2}$ teaspoon salt, and the plantains.

Bring to a boil, then reduce the heat to low and simmer until the plantains are tender, about 45 minutes.

Nestle the shrimp into the mixture in a single layer, cover, and cook just until the shrimp are cooked through, about 7 minutes. Season to taste with salt and pepper. Serve with hot sauce.

GULLAH-GEECHEE TRADITIONS

I want to rewrite the narrative of shrimp and grits here. I grew up with the shrimp and grits you probably know too—buttery, creamy, cheesy grits topped with saucy shrimp and sausage. That's what I thought they were. B.J. Dennis set me straight. He's a chef in Charleston reviving the Gullah-Geechee cooking of the sea islands along South Carolina's coast. Gullah-Geechee refers to the direct descendants of West and Central Africans who were enslaved on coastal plantations from Pender County, North Carolina, down to St. Johns County, Florida. With diverse African roots, they developed their own unique language, culture, art, and, of course, cuisine. After emancipation, they stayed and held on to their heritage. Isolated geographically, the Gullah-Geechee far outnumbered other residents. (That's been changing and continuing to change with real estate development.)

Traditionally, Gullah-Geechee farmed, fished, hunted, and bartered to make their own food, which is distinct from low-country cooking. B.J.'s family goes back eight generations in the Charleston islands, and he remembers his dad, uncles, and grandfather talking about crabbing and fishing. His family reminisces about cactus fruit juice, baked Awendaw, pulled molasses, palm fruit, muscadine grapes, red rice, shrimp pie, benne seed chutney, and groundnut cakes. B.J. says, "We ate what we grew and that's what we have to get back to."

Shrimp and grits are a prime example. The shrimp Carolina Gullahs caught and ate were creek shrimp, so sweet and tender, they were seasoned with nothing more than salt and pepper. They were simply cooked solo in their shells to create a gravy to spoon over grits. To make creamy grits without cream, dried corn kernels were smashed while simmering, releasing their sugary starches into the cooking liquid. Together, they were a light bowlful of natural sweetness from water and land.

I've dreamed and dreamed of that dish. I've imagined that maybe my South Carolina ancestors spooned up the same thing a century ago. You can't get those creek shrimp or the right type of dried corn anymore. (You can get good and true grits from Anson Mills, though. They're expensive, but worth ordering online.) I've done my best to capture the goodness of the original and to honor the cooks who created it.

Sea Island Shrimp and Grits

Everyday

Grits

1 cup stone-ground grits

1 bay leaf

Kosher salt and freshly
  ground black pepper

1 tablespoon fresh thyme
  leaves

Shrimp

2 tablespoons extra-virgin
  olive oil

1 pound large shrimp,
  peeled and deveined
  with tails on

Kosher salt and freshly
  ground black pepper

1/2 onion, diced

1 green bell pepper, seeded
  and finely diced

2 garlic cloves, thinly sliced

1 teaspoon chile flakes

2 plum tomatoes, cored and
  finely diced

3 tablespoons fresh flat-leaf
  parsley, chopped

To celebrate from-the-garden freshness, I've added aromatics and vegetables and herbs to my take on shrimp and grits. But I've kept out dairy, which isn't big in Gullah-Geechee cooking. You don't need it! Cream in grits is cheating. Yes, you have to stand over the stove and whisk for almost an hour, but your reward is silky grits. The only sauce here comes from the juices that the shrimp and tomatoes let out while cooking—and it's plenty to run in rivulets into the grits.

For the grits: Bring 4 1/2 cups water to a boil in a medium saucepan over medium heat. While whisking, add the grits in a slow, steady stream. Whisk in the bay leaf and 1 teaspoon salt. Reduce the heat to medium-low and continue whisking until the grits are thick and creamy, 40 to 45 minutes. Stir in the thyme leaves and 1 teaspoon black pepper. Season with salt. Cover and keep warm over very low heat, whisking occasionally. I like my grits loose, so I add water if they start to stiffen. You can too.

For the shrimp: Heat the oil in a large skillet over medium-high heat. Season the shrimp with salt and pepper. Working in batches, add the shrimp to the skillet and sear until just opaque, about 2 minutes per side. Transfer to a plate.

Reduce the heat to medium and add the onion and bell pepper. Cook, stirring occasionally, until softened, about 5 minutes. Add the garlic and chile flakes and cook, stirring, for 1 minute. Season with salt and pepper. Add the tomatoes and cook, gently folding, for 1 minute. Return the shrimp and any accumulated juices to the skillet and toss just until well combined.

Divide the grits among serving plates and top with the shrimp mixture. Garnish with the parsley and serve immediately.

Superfast Seafood Stew
WITH Fish AND Shrimp

SERVES 6	Everyday & Celebration

2 tablespoons unsalted butter

2 tablespoons all-purpose flour

1 tablespoon vegetable oil

2 andouille sausage links, thinly sliced

1 onion, diced

1 celery stalk, diced

1 poblano chile, seeded and diced

1 green bell pepper, seeded and diced

Kosher salt and freshly ground pepper

2 large garlic cloves, minced

2 fresh thyme sprigs

1 bay leaf

2 tablespoons Seafood Seasoning (page 240)

1 cup clam juice

1 ear corn, kernels cut, cob reserved

1 pound white fish fillets, cut into 2-inch chunks

1 pound shell-on deveined shrimp

Scallions, for garnish

Seafood doesn't come natural to me. I'm from landlocked Nashville, where fried catfish and canned salmon patties were all the seafood I knew growing up. Thankfully, I can turn to the soul food community for guidance. Charlotte Jenkins, chef-owner of her former restaurant, Gullah Cuisine, wrote the book—literally—on Gullah cuisine. She grew up in Awendaw, a fishing village near Charleston, South Carolina. "I miss the seafood from when I grew up," Charlotte recalls. "The fish and crab were so plentiful in the creek." She transformed that memory into one of her most popular dishes, Gullah rice. In it, she combines andouille sausage with carrots, peppers, onions, and, of course, shrimp.

Inspired by Charlotte's story and drawing on the gumbo I created while competing on *Top Chef*, I whipped up this seafood stew. It's a quick version that keeps the peppers and corn crisp and the fish and shrimp tender. This pretty pot would be at home on any weeknight or for a sit-down dinner party.

Melt the butter in a small saucepan over medium heat. Add the flour and cook, stirring often, until dark brown, about 10 minutes. Remove the roux from the heat.

Meanwhile, heat the oil in a large Dutch oven over medium heat. Add the sausage and cook, stirring often, until browned, 2 to 3 minutes. Transfer to a plate. Add the onion, celery, chile, bell pepper, and 1/2 teaspoon salt. Cook, stirring often, until just tender, about 5 minutes. Add the garlic and cook, stirring, for 3 minutes. Add the thyme, bay leaf, seafood seasoning, and 1/4 teaspoon black pepper. Cook, stirring, for 2 minutes.

Add the clam juice, 3 cups water, the corncob, and the browned sausage with any accumulated juices. Bring to a boil, then reduce the heat to simmer steadily. Stir in the roux, then simmer for 10 minutes. Discard the corncob, thyme sprigs, and bay leaf.

Fold in the fish and shrimp, making sure they're submerged in the liquid. Cover and simmer over medium heat, stirring occasionally, until just cooked through, about 7 minutes. Stir in the corn kernels.

Divide among bowls and garnish with scallions.

Cracked Shrimp with Comeback Sauce

SERVES 6	*Celebration*

2 cups all-purpose flour

2 tablespoons cornstarch

1 teaspoon paprika

Kosher salt and freshly ground black pepper

2 large eggs

1/2 cup evaporated milk

1/2 teaspoon minced fresh flat-leaf parsley, plus more for serving

2 pounds large shrimp, peeled and deveined, with tails left intact

Vegetable oil, for frying

Lemon wedges, for serving

Comeback Sauce (page 247), for serving

Usually, I can take or leave shrimp. But this dish? You better watch out, 'cause I could polish it all off. Skillet-fried shrimp stay hot and juicy in their golden crackly crust. They cool just enough after a dip in comeback sauce, an addictive mix that's Thousand Island meets rémoulade. The secret to this dish is the "cracking." When I was cooking as a private chef in the Bahamas, I learned how to crack conch. The notoriously tough local conch had to be pounded with a mallet to make it tender enough to eat. Shrimp have a texture that starts softer, so a little tap, tap with a rolling pin is enough to flatten and tenderize them. In that smashed state, they need only a quick dunk in bubbling oil to turn into the most delicious fried shrimp you'll ever eat.

Whisk the flour, cornstarch, paprika, 1 teaspoon salt, and 1/2 teaspoon pepper in a pie plate. Whisk the eggs in a large bowl until frothy, then whisk in the evaporated milk, parsley, 1/2 teaspoon salt, and 1/2 teaspoon pepper. Gently pound the shrimp with a rolling pin until cracked and flattened.

Fill a large cast-iron skillet with oil to a depth of 1/4 inch. Heat over medium-high heat until hot but not smoking. Dip a shrimp into the egg mixture, then dredge in the flour mixture, shake off excess, and slip into the hot oil. Repeat with enough shrimp to fill the skillet without crowding it. Fry, flipping once, until golden, about 1 minute per side. Drain on paper towels. Repeat with the remaining shrimp.

Transfer to a serving platter and garnish with parsley. Serve hot with lemon wedges for squeezing and comeback sauce for dipping.

Seasonings and Condiments

Poultry Seasoning

1 teaspoon dried sage

1 teaspoon dried thyme

1 teaspoon dried rosemary

¼ teaspoon dried oregano

¼ teaspoon celery seeds

⅛ teaspoon freshly grated
   nutmeg

Of course, you can sprinkle this over poultry before roasting, grilling, or panfrying. But it really works its magic in Spoonbread Dressing (page 149) or any stuffing or dressing. It makes the dish taste meaty even when it's meatless!

Pulse all the ingredients in a spice grinder until finely ground. Use immediately or seal in a jar for up to 1 month.

Seafood Seasoning

1½ teaspoons sweet paprika

1 teaspoon granulated garlic

1 teaspoon freshly ground black pepper

½ teaspoon celery seeds

½ teaspoon cayenne pepper

½ teaspoon dried thyme

½ teaspoon dried basil

½ teaspoon dried oregano

When it comes to seasoning, I'm a control freak. And I can't control the salt I'm adding to a dish with store-bought spice blends. Usually, it's the first ingredient, which leaves dishes way too salty. Plus, homemade blends end up fresher. It takes only a minute to make your own!

Mix all the ingredients together. Use immediately or seal in a jar for up to 1 month.

Barbecue Spice Blend

4 teaspoons ground cumin

4 teaspoons ground coriander

1 teaspoon garlic powder

½ teaspoon ground cardamom

¼ teaspoon cayenne pepper

1 teaspoon kosher salt

½ teaspoon freshly ground black pepper

Sprinkle this over any meat before grilling, smoking, or roasting. Cardamom's my secret weapon in this blend. Surprising and warming, it brings a rounded warmth to barbecue.

Mix all the spices together. Use immediately or seal in a jar for up to 1 month.

Piri Piri Spice

2¼ teaspoons sweet
 paprika

1½ teaspoons cayenne
 pepper

1½ teaspoons garlic
 powder

1½ teaspoons dried
 oregano

1½ teaspoons kosher salt

1 teaspoon confectioners'
 sugar

½ teaspoon ground
 cinnamon

½ teaspoon ground
 cardamom

¾ teaspoon chile flakes

¾ teaspoon ground ginger

Piri piri is a type of chile used in African and Portuguese hot spice blends and sauces. It's hard to find here, so I've replicated the taste with a blend of paprika, cayenne, and chile flakes.

Mix all the ingredients together. Use immediately or seal in a jar for up to 1 month.

Curry Powder

1 tablespoon ground
   coriander

1 tablespoon ground cumin

1 tablespoon ground
   turmeric

1 teaspoon ground ginger

½ teaspoon dry mustard

½ teaspoon ground
   cinnamon

¼ teaspoon ground
   cardamom

¼ teaspoon cayenne
   pepper

¼ teaspoon freshly ground
   black pepper

My husband, Matthew, makes the best curry. When I was catering, I'd come home too exhausted to lift a finger. Matthew would hand me a plate of his chicken curry and I'd feel so loved. This from-scratch mix is for him.

Mix all the ingredients together. Use immediately or seal in a jar for up to 1 month.

Harissa Spice Mix

½ teaspoon cumin seeds

½ teaspoon coriander
   seeds

⅛ teaspoon caraway or
   anise seeds

1 tablespoon chile flakes

½ teaspoon smoked
   paprika

¼ teaspoon garlic powder

¼ teaspoon kosher salt

Throughout North Africa, harissa sits on every table. It's a red chile paste stirred into nearly every dish. I've turned the sauce into a spice mix that tastes great on candied nuts (see page 26). It would make a nice grilling rub for meat too.

Combine the cumin, coriander, and caraway seeds in a small skillet and set over medium heat. Toast, stirring occasionally, until fragrant, 3 to 4 minutes. Let cool completely, then transfer to a spice grinder.

Add the chile flakes, smoked paprika, garlic powder, and salt. Grind to a fine powder. The spice mix will keep in an airtight container for up to 1 month.

Hot 'n' Zesty Broccoli Panko Crunch

2 cups finely chopped
  broccoli florets

1 cup whole wheat panko
  breadcrumbs

1½ tablespoons canola oil

½ teaspoon kosher salt

½ teaspoon chile flakes

¾ teaspoon fresh lemon
  zest

Crunchy breadcrumbs get even more delicious with charred bits of broc-coli. Spiked with chile and lemon zest, this topping is great on beans (see page 130), mac and cheese, and stews.

Preheat the oven to 450°F.

Toss the broccoli, panko, oil, salt, and chile flakes in a large bowl until well mixed. Spread the broccoli mixture evenly on a half-sheet pan.

Bake, stirring occasionally, until browned and crisp, about 10 minutes. Toss in the lemon zest and let cool completely. Use immediately.

Lemon-Thyme Benne

MAKES ABOUT ¼ CUP

¼ cup white sesame seeds

½ teaspoon dried thyme

½ teaspoon kosher salt

1 teaspoon freshly grated
   lemon zest

Benne seeds may sound like some fancy-pants ingredient, but they're actually white sesame seeds. Benne's the name for them in Gullah-Geechee cuisine. Members of the Gullah-Geechee community live along the coast from Jacksonville, North Carolina, to Jacksonville, Florida, with a big concentration in South Carolina and its sea islands. They are descended from the West African slaves in that region and have retained much of the language, culture, and traditions passed down from their ancestors. Amazing, right? Everything else around them is swirling with change and they've held tight to their heritage, especially their culinary one. Benne seeds figure prominently in the cooking, which is tied closely to the land, sea, and seasons. Inspired by the Gullah-Geechee, I showcase their beloved seeds in a lemon-thyme sprinkle that's lovely with roasted carrots (page 92) and tasty over any fresh, seasonal vegetables, fish, or poultry.

Heat the sesame seeds in a small skillet over medium heat, tossing occasionally, until golden brown, about 5 minutes. Remove from the heat and add the thyme and salt while the seeds are warm. Transfer to a dish and let cool completely, then toss in the lemon zest. Use immediately.

Barbecue Sauce

MAKES 2½ CUPS

2 tablespoons vegetable oil

¾ cup diced onion

2 teaspoons sliced garlic

1 serrano chile, minced and seeded if desired

Kosher salt

1¼ teaspoons ground cumin

½ teaspoon ground coriander

½ teaspoon freshly ground black pepper

3 tablespoons plus 1 teaspoon apple cider vinegar

1½ cups ketchup

1 tablespoon plus 1 teaspoon dark brown sugar

1 tablespoon molasses

1 tablespoon yellow mustard

This is my just-right sauce. Thin enough to brush on as a glaze and cook longer on the grill or in the oven. Thick enough to serve on its own. Sweet and spiced, tangy and hot. Smooth with just enough bitty bits to remind you how much better homemade tastes.

Heat the oil in a large saucepan over medium-low heat. Add the onion, garlic, chile, and ½ teaspoon salt. Cook, stirring occasionally, until the onion is translucent, about 8 minutes. Stir in the cumin, coriander, and black pepper. Add the vinegar and bring to a boil, then add the ketchup, brown sugar, molasses, mustard, and ¾ cup water.

Return to a boil, then reduce the heat to low and simmer, stirring occasionally, until the flavors have melded, about 15 minutes. Season with salt. Use immediately or refrigerate in jars for up to 2 weeks.

Pineapple-Habanero Hot Sauce

MAKES 1½ CUPS

15 Fresno chiles or other large hot red chiles, chopped

2 habanero chiles, chopped

1 cup chopped fresh pineapple

3 garlic cloves, chopped

1½ cups distilled white vinegar

1 teaspoon kosher salt

I got hot sauce in my bag. Yeah, that's a thing. Hot sauce is a pillar of soul food. And African-Americans did—and do—carry their own bottles sometimes. Sure, it's 'cause others' dishes need more flavor to match our heat. But there's a dark history too.

During Jim Crow, black people weren't allowed to dine alongside whites and in some cases were banned from sitting down at all. The restaurants would sell African-Americans food, but not allow us to eat on the premises. That meant that they had to bring their own condiments—and even their own plates and utensils. We didn't let Jim Crow stop us from enjoying food to the fullest. And I want us to relish hot sauce even now.

This homemade blend borrows from Caribbean ingredients that give it a fruity tartness under the fire. I created it for fried chicken (page 175), but it makes everything better, from Dirty Rice (page 192) to all vegetables. Consider yourself warned: this is boom-shakalaka hot. If you want a milder brew, cut out and discard all the seeds and ribs from the chiles.

Combine the chiles, pineapple, garlic, vinegar, and salt in a small saucepan. Bring to a boil over high heat. Boil until the chiles and pineapple are tender, 10 to 15 minutes. Remove from the heat.

Transfer to a blender and puree until very smooth. Pass through a fine-mesh sieve, pressing on the solids to extract all the sauce. Use immediately or refrigerate in jars for up to 2 weeks.

Comeback Sauce

1 cup mayonnaise

¼ cup chili sauce

¼ cup ketchup

2 tablespoons vegetable oil

1 tablespoon fresh lemon juice

2 teaspoons Worcestershire sauce

1 teaspoon hot sauce

1 garlic clove, grated on a Microplane

2 tablespoons grated onion

1 teaspoon brown mustard

½ teaspoon kosher salt

½ teaspoon freshly ground black pepper

Deep in the Mississippi Delta, the Alluvian seems to pop out of nowhere. This hotel in Greenwood anchors the corner of the one main street, single stoplight swinging at the intersection. It's actually owned and run by the Viking corporation, which builds its stoves in factories nearby. In the middle of our road trip for this book, my writer, Genevieve; my photographer, Gabriele; and I stopped here for a night. We ate at its restaurant, Giardina, where each table is in a Prohibition-era booth, with walls nearly up to the ceiling and a curtain "door" to enclose the space. Even with that setup, I think everyone in the restaurant could hear me when I screamed, "What?! Comeback sauce!"

Seeing that sauce on the menu brought back so many memories. Even though it's a Mississippi specialty, comeback sauce was a staple of my Nashville upbringing. With mayonnaise as its base, it gets spiced up with chili sauce, hot sauce, Worcestershire sauce, and garlic. I threw in a few of my other favorite seasonings to get the taste just right. You need this for dipping Cracked Shrimp (page 234). It's awesome with anything fried, as a salad dressing, for dipping chilled seafood, and, yes, saltine crackers.

Mix all the ingredients together until well blended. Use immediately or refrigerate in jars for up to 1 week.

Cranberry Sauce WITH Apples AND Ginger

1 (12-ounce) bag fresh or frozen cranberries, thawed if frozen

2 Granny Smith or other tart apples, peeled, cored, and cut into ½-inch chunks

½ cup sugar

½ cup unsweetened tart cherry juice or dry red wine

2 (3-inch) strips orange zest, removed with a vegetable peeler

2 teaspoons fresh grated peeled ginger

1 cinnamon stick

½ teaspoon kosher salt

I love a good pucker. Give me anything tart and I'm happy. That's why my Thanksgiving sauce combines all the tangy things: green apples, sour cherry juice, orange zest. If you're not as into zing as I am, you can use ¾ cup sugar.

Combine all the ingredients with ½ cup water in a medium saucepan. Bring to a boil over high heat, stirring to dissolve the sugar. Reduce the heat to maintain a simmer, and simmer until the cranberries have softened, about 20 minutes.

Let cool to room temperature before serving. Use immediately or refrigerate in jars for up to 2 weeks.

Chile-Lime Mango Jam

½ cup sugar

4 teaspoons fresh lime juice

¼ teaspoon chile flakes

⅛ teaspoon salt

2 mangoes, peeled, pitted, and diced

My ancestors jammed all the goods from this land—berries, stone fruits, peppers. I do too. But then I thought, "Why not take fruits from Africa and the Caribbean and put 'em up in the African-American jamming tradition?" So I did! And mango jam is delicious! This one uses lime juice to bring out the floral notes of the juicy fruit, and chile and salt to give it a hint of savory. That means you can slather it all over biscuits (pages 158 to 162) for a sweet treat and serve it with fish, chicken, or pork too.

Combine the sugar, lime juice, chile flakes, salt, half of the mangoes, and ½ cup water in a medium saucepan. Bring to a boil over high heat, stirring to dissolve the sugar. Reduce the heat to keep a simmer, and simmer, gently mashing the mangoes with a wooden spoon, until the mixture is thick, about 10 minutes.

Fold in the remaining mango and adjust the heat to get a simmer going. Simmer just until the fresh cubes get a little tender, about 8 minutes. You want to keep those chunks in there, but you also want to cook them enough so they don't weep into your jam later.

Divide the jam among jars and seal properly or refrigerate for up to 1 month.

Sorghum Butter

4 tablespoons (2 ounces) unsalted butter, very soft

1 teaspoon sorghum syrup

Pinch of salt

Sorghum syrup tastes like the love child of molasses and honey. I like to stir a little into butter to spread all over biscuits (pages 158 to 162). You can find it online and in some markets, or substitute honey.

Whisk the butter in a small bowl until smooth. Whisk in the sorghum and salt until fully incorporated. Use immediately.

Tangy Tomato Sauce

MAKES ABOUT 3 CUPS

2 tablespoons extra-virgin
olive oil

1 small onion, finely diced

Kosher salt and freshly
ground black pepper

2 garlic cloves, thinly sliced

1 (28-ounce) can whole
tomatoes

1 tablespoon unsalted
butter

Back to basics, folks. You don't need to add sugar to tomato sauce to sweeten it. You just need to let it cook, starting with caramelizing onions. I take this to the point where there's a nice tang to the tomatoes. We're not going for canned kiddy sauce here. At the end, I stir in a little bit of butter for some lactic love. It rounds out the sauce beautifully.

Heat the oil in a large saucepan over medium-low heat. Add the onion and 1 teaspoon salt and cook, stirring often, until caramelized, about 10 minutes. Add the garlic and cook, stirring often, until tender, about 5 minutes.

Crush the tomatoes with your hands and add to the saucepan, along with any sauce from the can. Stir in $1/4$ teaspoon pepper. Bring to a boil, then reduce the heat to maintain a steady simmer. Simmer until thickened, about 30 minutes. Stir in the butter until it melts and remove from the heat. Use immediately or refrigerate in an airtight container for up to 1 week.

Serrano Kale Pistou

MAKES ABOUT 1¼ CUPS

1 large garlic clove, thinly sliced

2 teaspoons apple cider vinegar

1 small serrano chile, thinly sliced

4 cups packed chopped kale

½ teaspoon kosher salt

½ cup canola–olive oil blend or ¼ cup canola oil mixed with ¼ cup extra-virgin olive oil

I had to cross the Atlantic to start cooking soul food on my own. As a model, I once lived in France and loved the local eats, but got so homesick for my comfort foods. Other models from the South missed the same classics, so I began cooking Sunday suppers for us with ingredients from the markets of Paris. Without even realizing it, I began to fuse the two cuisines. Not that I was the first one. Thomas Jefferson, America's founding Francophile, often served French food at Monticello. And who do you think was doing the cookin'? That's right. His African-American chef, James Hemings. As Jefferson's chef, Hemings prepared French cuisine and created his own Virginian-French style. He passed on his knowledge to all the other cooks, who often went on to cook in the same style on other plantations.

In homage to Hemings, I've converted a classic French herb topping into a mix with fall greens and Southern seasonings. Chile gives it a spicy kick, and vinegar takes the edge off the raw garlic while giving the mix that tang I'm always chasing in soul food. It's a great final sprinkle over any soup or stew, fat wedges of steamed cabbage, or roasted vegetables, and it can be mixed into pasta too.

Combine the garlic and vinegar in a small bowl. Let stand for 5 minutes while you prepare the remaining ingredients. Put the garlic with the vinegar, the chile, kale, and salt in a food processor. Pulse until the kale is very finely chopped. With the processor running, add the oil in a steady stream. Use immediately or refrigerate in an airtight container for up to 2 days.

Walnut Kale Pesto

Add ½ cup walnuts to the processor along with the remaining solid ingredients.

Harvest Chow Chow

2 cups finely chopped purple cabbage

4 cups finely chopped green cabbage

2 cups finely diced red onion

2 cups finely diced peeled beets

1 cup finely diced peeled celery root

1 cup finely diced peeled turnips

$\frac{1}{2}$ cup finely diced jalapeño chiles

$\frac{1}{3}$ cup kosher salt

2 cups apple cider vinegar

1 cup water

$\frac{1}{2}$ cup sugar

2 tablespoons yellow mustard seeds

$1\frac{1}{2}$ teaspoons ground turmeric

1 teaspoon celery seeds

At the end of the summer harvest, gardeners, farmers, and cooks all over the South chop cabbage, peppers, and green tomatoes to pickle into chow chow relish. I wondered what would happen if I did the same with fall's bounty. The blend of root vegetables—beets, celery root, turnips—mellow out the cabbage relish with their earthy mildness. Unlike its zingy summer cousin, this chow chow is chill. It still has a bright pop, perfect for topping soups, stews, and hearty meat braises. Of course, it's also great over hot dogs and sandwiches.

Mix both cabbages, the onion, beets, celery root, turnips, jalapeños, and salt in a large bowl, using your hands. Cover and refrigerate overnight.

Transfer the mixture to a large colander and rinse and drain well before returning to the bowl.

Combine the vinegar, water, sugar, mustard seeds, turmeric, and celery seeds in a medium saucepan. Bring to a boil over medium-high heat, stirring to dissolve the sugar. Pour over the vegetables and stir well. Divide among canning jars and properly seal the jars or simply refrigerate them. The chow chow will keep for up to 6 months in the refrigerator.

Red Onion Pickles

1 large red onion, halved and very thinly sliced

1 habanero chile, split in half

1 fresh or dried bay leaf

½ cup apple cider vinegar

1 teaspoon sugar

½ teaspoon kosher salt

On our little kitchen table in Nashville, we always kept a little jar of home-made pickles. Now, it wasn't anything fancy. Mama'd drop some sliced onions or peppers into the jar and pour vinegar over them. That was it. But it was enough to pucker up those suckers. We'd spoon them over all our dishes, enjoying their light tang and crunch on day one, their soft whoo-dang! tart bite on day two. I've kept up that tradition, always ready to douse anything with soul food's signature pucker. Open up my fridge and you'll always find all types of pickled things. One constant is pickled onions. They go with everything—and I mean everything. I created these to dress Green Bean Salad (page 57), but I also put them in sandwiches and burgers and over hot dogs, eggs, beans, fish, and meat. Sometimes I even eat them by the forkful.

Pack the onion, chile, and bay leaf in a half-pint jar. Add the vinegar, sugar, and salt. Cover the jar tightly and shake well. The vinegar won't cover the onion mixture at first, but the onions will wilt over time and end up immersed in liquid. Refrigerate for at least 4 hours or up to 1 week, shaking occasionally.

Pickled Delicata Squash

Kosher salt

2 small delicata squash, trimmed, seeded, and cut into 1-inch rings

$\frac{1}{2}$ cup red wine vinegar

$\frac{1}{2}$ cup apple cider vinegar

$\frac{1}{2}$ cup water

$\frac{1}{4}$ cup sugar

1 cinnamon stick

2 whole cloves

5 whole allspice berries

Delicata squash, not as starchy as butternut and sweeter than acorn, develop a nice bite after pickling. Plus, their cylindrical shape stacks easily in canning jars.

Bring a large saucepan of generously salted water to a boil. Add the squash and boil for 2 minutes. Drain and pack into pint jars.

Combine both vinegars, the water, sugar, cinnamon, cloves, and allspice in a medium saucepan and bring to a boil over medium-high heat, stirring to dissolve the sugar. Pour over the squash in the jars to cover. Seal the jars to can properly, or simply put on the lids and refrigerate for up to 6 months.

Pickled Beets

1 cup red wine vinegar

1 cup apple cider vinegar

$1/2$ cup sugar

$1/4$ cup grated peeled fresh horseradish

10 whole cloves

1 teaspoon black peppercorns

4 cups 1-inch chunks peeled beets

Horseradish has a peppery hot bite that balances the sugariness of earthy beets. This pickling liquid would be delicious poured over sliced carrots, cauliflower florets, or cut green beans too.

Combine both vinegars, the sugar, horseradish, cloves, peppercorns, and 1 cup water in a large saucepan and bring to a boil, stirring to dissolve the sugar. Add the beets and stir well. Divide among jars and can properly, or simply seal the jars and refrigerate for at least 2 days or up to 2 months.

Mustard Corn Relish

½ cup white vinegar

½ cup sugar

2 tablespoons mustard seeds

1 teaspoon mustard powder

¼ teaspoon ground turmeric

2 teaspoons kosher salt

1 teaspoon freshly ground black pepper

2 cups fresh corn kernels

1 cup finely diced red bell pepper

¼ cup diced onion

1 red finger chile, minced

Plumped mustard seeds pop with each spoonful of this hot, tart, and sweet topping. I love it on hot dogs and meaty sandwiches, over grilled or roasted vegetables, and scattered over salads and soups.

Combine the vinegar, sugar, mustard seeds, mustard powder, turmeric, salt, black pepper, and ¾ cup water in a medium saucepan and bring to a boil, stirring to dissolve the sugar. Add the corn, bell pepper, onion, and chile. Boil, stirring occasionally, for 10 minutes.

Divide among jars and can properly, or simply seal the jars and refrigerate for up to 2 weeks.

Inspiration surrounds us – the trick is in knowing how to build flavors that tell the story you want to share.

Desserts

GROWING ORGANIC

In 1874, Jupiter Gilliard, born a slave in South Carolina, acquired a farm in Brunswick, Georgia. In 2010, six generations later, Matthew Raiford moved back home to Brunswick to take over Gilliard Farms.

He says, "From the time I left in 1985, I only ever came back for deaths and marriages. There was nothing for me in the South. I grew up with racism every day and was happy to move away." But when his Grandma Nana deeded him and his sister the land, he knew it was time to go home.

With a vision of turning it into an organic farm, Matthew took classes in sustainable land management in California. When he got home, neighboring old farmers told him, "Boy, you ain't doing nothing new." Matthew quickly realized how right they were. When it came to chasing off the mosquito-spraying trucks and figuring out how to let the crops grow wild, Nana taught him 98 percent of what he needed to know.

Even her kitchen lessons have stayed with Matthew, who cooks professionally at a resort on St. Simons Island. The one he treasures most is her trick for sweet potato pie. For years, he wondered why her pie was better than all the others. Shortly before her passing, she finally divulged her secret. Just before the custard was done, she brushed on a final sheen of evaporated milk. It's a jewel he'll hold and pass on to future generations too.

Sweet Potato Pie

2 pounds sweet potatoes

1 disk Carla's Classic Pie Dough (page 275), fitted into a deep-dish pie plate and frozen

$1/2$ teaspoon ground cinnamon

$1/2$ teaspoon ground ginger

$1/4$ teaspoon ground allspice

$1/4$ teaspoon freshly grated nutmeg

$1/2$ teaspoon salt

5 tablespoons unsalted butter, softened

$1/2$ cup packed light brown sugar, plus more if needed

1 cup evaporated milk

2 large eggs

Custardy and classic, this easy pie shows off the earthy richness of sweet potatoes with a little butter and a blend of warming spices. Be sure to start with good-looking spuds—firm and speckle-free. As they bake, they'll caramelize a bit. Because sweet potatoes vary in sweetness, I have you taste the filling before beating in the eggs to see if you want a touch more sugar.

Preheat the oven to 350°F.

Put the sweet potatoes on a foil-lined half-sheet pan. Bake, turning once, until very tender, $1^{1}/2$ to 2 hours. When cool enough to handle, take the sweet potatoes out of their jackets and scrape the flesh into a 1-quart measuring cup. You should have $2^{1}/2$ cups packed sweet potato.

Raise the oven temperature to 425°F.

Line the frozen dough with foil and fill with pie weights. Bake until dry and set, about 25 minutes. Remove the foil with the weights and bake the dough until golden brown, about 5 minutes longer. Let cool completely, then place on a half-sheet pan.

Transfer the sweet potato to a large bowl and add the cinnamon, ginger, allspice, nutmeg, salt, butter, brown sugar, and the evaporated milk. Beat with a heavy whisk until smooth. Taste and add more brown sugar if you'd like. The amount will depend on the sweetness of your spuds. Add the eggs and whisk until fully incorporated. Pour into the pie crust and spread evenly.

Bake for 15 minutes, then reduce the oven temperature to 350°F. Bake until the top is golden brown and the filling has puffed and set, about 40 minutes. Let cool completely on a wire rack.

Make ahead: The unbaked crust can be frozen for up to 1 month. The sweet potatoes can be baked, mashed, and refrigerated for up to 3 days.

Pecan Pie

1 disk Carla's Classic Pie Dough (page 275), fitted into a deep-dish pie plate and frozen

2 tablespoons unsalted butter, softened

½ cup packed light brown sugar

3 large eggs, beaten

1 cup dark corn syrup

1 tablespoon apple cider vinegar

½ teaspoon salt

1 tablespoon bourbon

1 teaspoon pure vanilla extract

2 cups chopped pecans, toasted

Of course you want this for Thanksgiving, but it's great any time of year. An almost oozy butterscotch custard with toasted pecans gets a shot of vinegar to balance the sweetness. And a shot of bourbon too. That bit of booze deepens the buttery brown sugar blend. And its oaky scent takes me right back to Granny's. After a long day, she'd fix herself a drink at her barrel-shaped bar. Strolling around the living room, she'd swirl and clink the ice in her black-and-gold-striped highball glass or one of her brightly colored tin cocktail cups, unwinding with each sip of her bourbon. I don't drink, so this pie is my way of taking the edge off when life gets crazy. Each bite will make you feel as good as any drink.

Preheat the oven to 425°F.

Line the frozen dough with foil and fill with pie weights. Bake until dry and set, about 25 minutes. Remove the foil with the weights and bake the dough until golden brown, about 5 minutes longer. Let cool completely, then place on a half-sheet pan.

Reduce the oven temperature to 350°F.

Cream the butter and brown sugar with an electric mixer fitted with the paddle attachment or by hand with a wooden spoon until smooth and fluffy. While beating, add the eggs in a steady stream, then beat in the corn syrup, vinegar, salt, bourbon, and vanilla until smooth. Fold in the pecans and pour into the cooled pie shell.

Bake until golden brown and mostly set but still a bit jiggly, about 45 minutes. Cool completely on a wire rack.

Make ahead: The unbaked crust can be frozen for up to 1 month.

Blackberry Peach Crumble Pie

MAKES ONE 9-INCH PIE

1 disk Carla's Classic Pie Dough (page 275)

¼ teaspoon ground cinnamon

All-purpose flour, for rolling

½ cup sugar

1 tablespoon grated peeled fresh ginger

Zest and juice of 1 small lemon

2 tablespoons cornstarch

3 ripe large peaches, peeled, pitted, and cut into 1-inch chunks

3 cups blackberries

Do a little dance for this pie. Go on now. I did a shimmy after a slice because it's just so yummy. A little ginger gives peaches and berries a hot zing. Get the most fragrant, ripest fruit you can find and you'll end up with the juiciest filling. Don't be embarrassed to give those babies a little squeeze at the farm stand. The peaches should yield when you press them and the blackberries should feel heavy like they might burst.

Arrange a rack on the lowest level of the oven and preheat the oven to 450°F.

Cut off one quarter of the pie dough and break it into pebbly crumbles with some almond-size pieces. Toss with the cinnamon until evenly coated and refrigerate.

Roll the remaining dough on a lightly floured surface with a lightly floured rolling pin into a 12-inch round. Fit into a 9-inch pie plate and crimp the edges. Freeze until ready to fill.

Mix the sugar, ginger, lemon zest and juice, and cornstarch in a large bowl. Add the peaches and blackberries and toss until evenly coated. Pour into the rolled crust and spread evenly. Scatter the pie dough crumbles all over the top. Place the pie on a half-sheet pan and place on the lowest oven rack.

Bake until the crust is golden brown and the filling is bubbling, about 45 minutes. Let cool completely on a wire rack.

Nutmeg Eggnog Buttermilk Pie

SERVES 12

1 tablespoon all-purpose flour, plus more for rolling

1 disk Carla's Classic Pie Dough (page 275)

1¼ cups sugar

2 teaspoons freshly grated nutmeg

½ teaspoon salt

5 tablespoons unsalted butter, melted

3 large eggs

1 cup buttermilk

1 tablespoon golden rum

1 teaspoon pure vanilla extract

Every Christmas, Granny baked once-a-year treats that became family favorites. We'd each get pretty little etched glasses of boiled custard, her version of eggnog. Instead of drinking it, we'd dunk in wedges of her pound cake. After that, we'd each get nice slices of her buttermilk pie. This easy nutmeg-laced pie fuses those memories into one luscious dessert.

On a lightly floured surface, using a lightly floured rolling pin, roll the disk of dough from the center to the top, then rotate the disk a quarter turn and roll again. Keep rolling and turning to form a 12-inch round. Transfer to a 9-inch pie plate and press into the bottom and sides of the plate without stretching the dough. Gently tuck the overhang under the dough around the rim so that the edge is flush with the rim of the plate, then decoratively crimp. Freeze until firm, at least 10 minutes.

Preheat the oven to 425°F.

Line the dough with foil, then fill with dried beans. Bake on a half-sheet pan until the bottom of the dough is dry, about 25 minutes. You can check by carefully lifting one side of the foil to peek at the crust. If it looks dry and not at all shiny, carefully remove the weights with the foil. Return the crust to the oven and bake until golden brown, about 5 minutes. Transfer the crust to a wire rack.

While letting the crust cool slightly, make the filling: In a large bowl, whisk together the sugar, flour, nutmeg, and salt until well blended, then whisk in the butter until evenly moistened. Whisk in the eggs, then whisk in the buttermilk, rum, and vanilla until well blended. Pour into the warm crust.

Bake until the custard is almost set in the center and the top is golden brown, about 45 minutes. Let cool completely in the pie plate on a wire rack. Serve at room temperature.

Make ahead: The unbaked crust can be frozen for up to 1 month.

Carla's Classic Pie Dough

MAKES TWO 9-INCH CRUSTS

1 tablespoon sugar

1/2 teaspoon table salt

2 1/4 cups all-purpose flour, plus more for rolling

1 cup (8 ounces) cold unsalted butter, cut into 1/2-inch cubes

My go-to formula will give you a buttery no-fail crust. For the flakiest results, make sure all the ingredients are cold.

Dissolve the sugar and salt in 1/3 cup water and chill until cold.

Pulse the flour and butter in a food processor until the mixture looks like coarse meal with some pea-size pieces. Add the water all at once and pulse until the dough almost forms a ball. Divide the dough in half and flatten into two disks.

Wrap each disk tightly in plastic wrap and chill until firm, at least 30 minutes or up to 1 day.

Make ahead: You can freeze the dough for up to 3 months. Thaw overnight in the refrigerator before rolling.

Plum Cobbler

Filling

3^1/$_2$ pounds plums, pitted and cut into ^{1}/$_2$-inch chunks

2 tablespoons fresh lemon juice

^{1}/$_2$ cup packed light brown sugar

^{1}/$_4$ cup granulated sugar

2 tablespoons cornstarch

1 teaspoon apple cider vinegar

^{1}/$_2$ teaspoon ground cinnamon

^{1}/$_4$ teaspoon salt

Topping

^{2}/$_3$ cup all-purpose flour

1 tablespoon light brown sugar

^{3}/$_4$ teaspoon baking powder

^{1}/$_4$ teaspoon baking soda

^{1}/$_4$ teaspoon salt

1^1/$_2$ teaspoons trans-fat-free vegetable shortening

2 tablespoons cold unsalted butter, cut up

^{1}/$_2$ cup buttermilk

^{1}/$_2$ teaspoon sesame seeds

I love me some plums! It's 'cause I love anything tart. To bring out the fruit's tang, I throw in a dash of lemon juice and vinegar. Don't worry—the filling doesn't end up sour. That extra acid makes those plum beauties sing. Try to get a variety of plums so the cobbler ends up with a range of textures and flavors. The sesame-flecked drop biscuit topping stands up to the jammy filling, which is even better with a scoop of melting ice cream on top.

Preheat the oven to 375°F.

For the filling: Toss the plums, lemon juice, brown sugar, granulated sugar, cornstarch, vinegar, cinnamon, and salt in a large bowl until well mixed. Transfer to a large cast-iron skillet.

For the topping: Whisk the flour, brown sugar, baking powder, baking soda, and salt in a medium bowl. Add the shortening and rub it in with your fingers until the mixture resembles coarse meal. Add the butter and cut it in with a pastry cutter or your fingers until incorporated with a few pea-size pieces remaining. Add the buttermilk and fold in until the dry ingredients are evenly moistened.

Drop heaping spoonfuls of the topping mixture onto the plums, spacing them 1 inch apart. Sprinkle the topping with the sesame seeds.

Bake until the topping is golden brown and the filling is bubbling, about 45 minutes. Serve hot or warm with ice cream, if you'd like.

Banana Pudding

Pudding

¹/₄ cup cornstarch

³/₄ cup sugar

6 large egg yolks

¹/₄ teaspoon salt

1¹/₂ cups whole milk

¹/₂ cup half-and-half

¹/₂ cup mashed ripe banana

2 teaspoons pure vanilla extract

1 tablespoon unsalted butter

2 cups heavy cream

2 ripe bananas, cut into ¹/₂-inch chunks

If soul food had a signature dessert, this would be it. Layers of buttery cookies, banana slices in custardy pudding, and a fluffy vanilla topper meld into a big ol' hug of a dessert. Everyone who tastes my banana pudding says, "You've taken me back!" One woman looked me right in the eye with tears in hers and told me, "It's heaven." *That* is why I make this.

Instead of just folding banana slices into my pudding, I blend the fruit into the mix too. That double dose! Instead of the usual whipped cream topping, I make a meringue and torch the top for a campfire marshmallow effect. Yes, I did. My favorite twist? Keeping some cookies on the side so you get a buttery crunch with each bite.

You can assemble the whole thing in a big ol' pan like they do for church suppers and family reunions. I prefer giving each person her own cup. That way, there are no kids clashing spoons to see who can scoop more, no hot mess left in the pan. There are just lots of happy folks, tasting a bit of heaven.

For the pudding: Whisk the cornstarch, sugar, egg yolks, and salt in a medium bowl. Heat the milk, half-and-half, and mashed banana in a medium saucepan over medium heat until bubbles begin to form around the edges. While whisking the egg yolks, add the hot milk a little at a time. When the bowl feels warm, whisk in the remaining milk and whisk well.

Return to the saucepan and set over medium heat. Whisk until the custard thickens and then boils for 2 minutes. Put the vanilla and butter in a large bowl and strain the hot cream over them through a fine-mesh sieve. Stir until smooth, then press a piece of plastic wrap directly on the surface and refrigerate until cold.

Whisk the cream in a large bowl until soft peaks form. Whisk one third of the whipped cream into the pastry cream to loosen it, then gently fold in the remainder until incorporated. Fold in the banana chunks.

Continued

Meringue

6 large egg whites

1 cup plus 2 tablespoons sugar

¹/₂ teaspoon pure vanilla extract

1¹/₂ teaspoons apple cider vinegar

Vanilla Shortbread (page 281)

For the meringue: Whisk the egg whites and the sugar in the bowl of an electric mixer set over a saucepan of simmering water until the sugar dissolves and the mixture is warm to the touch. Immediately transfer to the mixer fitted with the whisk attachment and whisk on medium-high speed until shiny, stiff peaks form. The bowl should no longer feel warm. Whisk in the vanilla and vinegar.

Preheat the broiler.

Place 12 ramekins on a half-sheet pan. Crumble one cookie into the bottom of each. Divide the pudding among the ramekins, then top with the meringue. Broil until golden brown. Stick 2 shortbreads into each ramekin and serve immediately.

Vanilla Shortbread

3 cups all-purpose flour

$^3/_4$ teaspoon salt

$1^1/_2$ cups (12 ounces) unsalted butter, softened

$^3/_4$ cup sugar

1 tablespoon pure vanilla extract

Simple pleasure. That's what this is. A buttery little bite that's crunchy and crumbly. I use it in Banana Pudding (page 279), but it's delicious on its own too. My shortcut to shortbread? Pack the dough into a resealable plastic bag. No messy rolling or gaping holes in a dough log. Pressing the dough into the bag makes a nice even layer that's easy to store and cut.

Whisk the flour and salt in a medium bowl. Beat the butter and sugar in a mixer fitted with the paddle attachment on medium speed until creamy. Beat in the vanilla until incorporated.

Reduce the speed to low and gradually add the flour mixture. Beat, scraping the bowl occasionally, until the dough comes together in large clumps.

Transfer the dough to a gallon-size resealable plastic freezer bag and press into a 1-inch-thick, 9 by 5-inch rectangle. The bag is 9 inches wide, so you're pressing the dough to the edges. Refrigerate until firm, at least 2 hours and up to 2 days.

When ready to bake, preheat the oven to 350°F. Line cookie sheets with parchment paper.

Cut the dough into thirds to form rectangular logs that are 3 inches wide. Cut each log into $^1/_4$-inch-thick slices. Place the slices on the prepared sheet, spacing them $^1/_2$ inch apart.

Bake one sheet at a time until the edges are browned and the tops are golden, 14 to 18 minutes. Let cool completely on the sheets on wire racks.

Make ahead: The shortbread keeps at room temperature in an airtight container for up to 2 weeks.

Oatmeal Raisin Cookie Sandwiches with Buttercream Filling

Oatmeal Raisin Cookies

3/4 cup all-purpose flour

1/2 teaspoon ground cinnamon

3/4 teaspoon salt

1/4 teaspoon baking soda

8 tablespoons (4 ounces) unsalted butter, softened, butter wrapper reserved

1 cup packed light brown sugar

1 large egg, beaten

1 teaspoon pure vanilla extract

1 1/2 cups old-fashioned oats

1/2 cup raisins, chopped if large

Buttercream Filling

1/4 cup plus 2 teaspoons granulated sugar

2 large egg whites

1 cup (8 ounces) unsalted butter, cut into tablespoons and softened

1/4 teaspoon pure vanilla extract

Grandma Thelma, my dad's mom, used to buy crunchy oatmeal cookies coated with icing. Remember those? I loved those things! She used to slip them into my lunch bag. Now Granny, my mom's mom, used to make soft oatmeal raisin cookies that folks, family, *and* friends just couldn't get enough of. Instead of messing with memories, I created my own take, sandwiching a buttercream frosting between soft and chewy oatmeal raisin cookies. Of course, the cookies are tasty on their own too!

For the cookies: Preheat the oven to 325°F. Line 2 large cookie sheets with parchment paper.

Whisk the flour, cinnamon, salt, and baking soda in a small bowl. Beat the butter and brown sugar in a large bowl until creamed together. Add the egg and vanilla and beat until well mixed. The mixture may look broken. Add the flour mixture and fold until evenly moistened, then add the oats and raisins. Fold until evenly distributed.

Drop the dough by heaping tablespoons onto the prepared pans, spacing the rounds 2 inches apart. Use the reserved butter wrapper to push the rounds flat to a 1/2-inch thickness.

Bake one sheet at a time until the cookies are golden brown, 10 to 12 minutes. Place the sheets on wire racks and let cool completely.

For the filling: Put the granulated sugar and egg whites in a heatproof bowl and set over a saucepan of simmering water. Whisk until the sugar is dissolved and the mixture is warm to the touch.

Remove from the heat and immediately whisk with an electric mixer until stiff peaks form. While whisking, add the butter 1 tablespoon at a time and beat until incorporated. Whisk in the vanilla. If the mixture looks broken, whisk in 1 tablespoon warm water. Beat until creamy, adding another table-spoon warm water if needed for the frosting to come together.

Divide the buttercream among the flat sides of half the cookies and sand-wich with the remaining cookies. Refrigerate until the filling is set.

Make ahead: The unfilled cookies keep at room temperature in an air-tight container for up to 1 week. The filled cookies can be refrigerated for up to 3 days.

Chocolate Pound Cake

1 pound unsalted butter, cut into cubes, at room temperature, plus more for the pan

3½ cups all-purpose flour, plus more for the pan

1 cup unsweetened cocoa powder

1 teaspoon baking powder

1 teaspoon salt

6 large eggs, at room temperature

2 cups granulated sugar

1 cup packed light brown sugar

1 tablespoon pure vanilla extract

1 cup buttermilk

1 cup mini chocolate chips

Granny gave me her cherished pound cake recipe. And her blessing to make the recipe my own. That's the beauty of passing down recipes in the family. The details are meant to change with each generation, but the spirit stays the same. In the case of this cake, I found inspiration in generations before Granny. I saw a recipe in an old cookbook that started the batter in a cold oven. After trying that technique, I never turned back. It gives the cake an incredible short, dense crumb. The slow rise yields a center nearly as creamy as a chocolate truffle. The cocoa deepens over days even as the cake stays moist, making this ideal for shipping to loved ones far away or baking ahead of time for a party.

Butter and flour a 10-inch tube pan.

Sift the flour, cocoa powder, baking powder, and salt into a large bowl. Break the eggs into a separate bowl. Beat the butter with both sugars in a stand mixer with the paddle attachment on low speed until blended. Scrape the bowl, raise the speed to medium, and beat until really creamy.

Scrape the bowl, turn the speed to medium, and add the eggs one at a time, beating really well after each addition. Scrape the bowl, add the vanilla, and beat again on medium speed until well blended.

With the speed on low, gradually add the dry ingredients in thirds, alternating with the buttermilk. Scrape the bowl, add the chocolate chips, and mix just until blended. Pour into the prepared pan and smooth the top.

Put the pan in the center of a cold oven and turn the heat to 325°F. Bake until a tester or skewer comes out clean, about 1 hour and 45 minutes. Let cool in the pan on a wire rack for 30 minutes, then unmold and let cool completely on the rack.

Make ahead: The cake keeps at room temperature tightly wrapped for up to 1 week.

Poured Caramel Cake

8 tablespoons (4 ounces)
   unsalted butter

1¾ cups sugar

½ teaspoon salt

1 (12-ounce) can evaporated
   milk

Yellow Sheet Cake
   (page 288)

For years, I chased the perfect caramel cake recipe. It's not so much about the taste and texture as about the feeling that hits with the first bite. To get the right sensation, the caramel needs to be silky soft and sticky, creamy yet dark, pourable but not thin or runny. And the cake should be fine-grained and light yet sturdy enough to stand up to a caramel cloak. That's what this recipe is! Growing up, I had countless versions—three-layer towers and double stacks. But I prefer a nice, thick sheet cake to balance the sweetness of the caramel, which runs down the sides of every slice so there's still plenty to go around. Bring this to any party and the crowd will go wild.

Set the butter in a large pot over medium heat. When it's halfway melted, add the sugar and salt. Cook, stirring with a wooden spoon, until the mixture is dark golden brown. It will look grainy and the fat will separate from the sugar and then come back together.

Remove from the heat and add the evaporated milk while whisking. Be careful! The caramel will bubble up. Scrape up any sugar that's stuck to the bottom of the pan. Make sure the sugar is completely dissolved.

Set over low heat and cook, whisking often, until very smooth and creamy, about 1 hour. Remove from the heat and let cool completely, stirring occasionally.

When ready to serve, pour the caramel all over the cake.

Yellow Sheet Cake

MAKES ONE 9 BY13 BY 2-INCH CAKE

6 tablespoons unsalted butter, cut into tablespoons and softened, plus more for the pan

2 cups all-purpose flour, plus more for the pan

3/4 cup buttermilk

1 teaspoon pure vanilla extract

1 1/4 cups sugar

2 teaspoons baking powder

1/2 teaspoon salt

2 tablespoons vegetable oil

3 large eggs, at room temperature

At casual Southern gatherings—book clubs and prayer meetings and such—ladies come toting sheet cakes. They're all nestled in their pans, usually Pyrex, and ready to have fat squares cut right out of them. They're the warmest welcome. Neither fussy nor fancy, but always yummy. This yellow vanilla cake tastes good enough to serve plain with tea, but you can pour caramel all over it too (see page 287).

Preheat the oven to 350°F. Butter and flour a 9 by 13-inch cake pan.

Combine the buttermilk and vanilla in a medium bowl. Combine the flour, the sugar, baking powder, and salt in the bowl of a stand mixer. Beat with the paddle attachment on low speed until well mixed. Add the oil and beat until evenly distributed. With the machine running, add the butter 1 tablespoon at a time and beat until fully incorporated. The mixture will look like coarse sand.

Add the eggs one at a time, beating well after each addition and scraping the bowl occasionally. While beating, add the buttermilk mixture in a slow, steady stream. Beat just until smooth. Pour the batter into the prepared pan and spread evenly.

Bake until a tester inserted in the center comes out clean, about 25 minutes. Let cool completely in the pan on a wire rack.

Make ahead: The cake keeps at room temperature covered tightly for up to 3 days.

Gingerbread Layer Cake ⊞ Lemon Cream Cheese Frosting

SERVES 12

Gingerbread Cake

- 4 tablespoons (2 ounces) unsalted butter, softened, plus more for the pans
- 2 cups all-purpose flour
- 1⅓ cups packed dark brown sugar
- 1 tablespoon baking powder
- 1 teaspoon salt
- 2 teaspoons ground cinnamon
- 2 teaspoons ground ginger
- 2 teaspoons freshly grated nutmeg
- ½ teaspoon ground cloves
- 3 large eggs, at room temperature
- 2 large egg yolks, at room temperature
- ⅔ cup molasses
- 2 teaspoons pure vanilla extract
- ⅓ cup hot water
- ½ cup buttermilk
- ⅓ cup canola oil

Go all out for Christmas. This cake combines the warmth of wintry ginger-bread with a lemony frosting that tastes like sunshine. When I made this for my family, my nieces and nephews went crazy over it. It was the best gift I could've given them.

To make the cake: Preheat the oven to 375°F. Butter three 8-inch round cake pans, line with parchment paper, and butter the parchment.

Sift the flour, brown sugar, baking powder, salt, cinnamon, ginger, nutmeg, and cloves into the bowl of an electric mixer fitted with the paddle attach-ment. In a medium bowl, whisk the eggs, egg yolks, molasses, and vanilla. In a small bowl, stir together the hot water and buttermilk.

Mix the dry ingredients on low speed until well blended. Add the 4 table-spoons butter and the oil and continue mixing on low until the mixture re-sembles fine crumbs. With the machine running, add the egg mixture and beat just until incorporated, then add the buttermilk mixture in a steady stream. Scrape down the bottom and sides of the bowl and mix again just until evenly combined. Divide the batter evenly among the three pre-pared pans.

Bake until a cake tester comes out clean, 20 to 25 minutes. When you lightly touch the top of the cake, it should feel a little bouncy but still show the indentation of your finger. Let cool in the pans on wire racks for 10 minutes. Unmold the cakes and place top side up on the racks. Let cool completely.

Continued

Lemon Frosting

2 tablespoons freshly
   grated lemon zest

¾ cup fresh lemon juice

¾ cup granulated sugar

3 large egg yolks

10 tablespoons unsalted
   butter, cut into
   tablespoons

2 (8-ounce) blocks cream
   cheese, softened

Confectioners' sugar
   (optional)

To make the lemon frosting: Whisk the lemon zest and juice, granulated sugar, egg yolks, and 6 tablespoons of the butter in a medium saucepan over medium-high heat until bubbles begin to form around the edges of the pan, about 3 minutes. Reduce the heat to medium-low and stir continuously with a spatula until thick enough to coat the spatula, about 10 minutes. Strain through a fine-mesh sieve into a large bowl.

Stir in the remaining 4 tablespoons butter, 1 tablespoon at a time, letting each addition melt before adding the next. Press plastic wrap directly against the surface and refrigerate until cold and stiff.

Beat the cream cheese by hand in a large bowl just until smooth. Whisk the lemon curd to loosen it, then add to the cream cheese. Fold until well combined.

To assemble the cake: Place one cake layer, bottom side up, on a cake plate. Spread one third of the lemon cream evenly on top, leaving a 1-inch rim, and gently press another cake layer, bottom side up, on top. Spread half of the remaining lemon cream on its top, leaving a 1-inch rim; then top with the final cake layer, top side up. You can either dust with confectioners' sugar and serve with the remaining lemon cream or spread the remaining cream on top. Refrigerate until set, at least 2 hours.

Make ahead: The cake layers keep at room temperature tightly wrapped for up to 2 days. The lemon curd can be refrigerated for up to 2 days. The assembled cake can be refrigerated for up to 1 day.

Coconut Cream Layer Cake

MAKES ONE 11 BY 5-INCH LAYER CAKE

4 cups unsweetened
    coconut flakes

3 cups sour cream

1½ cups sugar

⅛ teaspoon salt

Coconut Cake (page 294)

You've never seen a coconut cake like this before! Okay, well, maybe you have. But the only place I ever had it was at my childhood friend Karen's house. We usually had a slice after several rounds of a card game called canasta. In place of the usual seven-minute frosting, her mom, Ginny, mixed sour cream with shredded coconut. That's my jam because I like the tang. After years of tinkering with proportions, I've hit on a mix that's creamy and coconutty with a hint of tart to balance the sweetness. The hardest part of this one-bowl dump-and-stir frosting is not rushing it—it needs to hang out in the fridge so that the coconut softens and the mix stiffens enough to spread. Trust me, it's worth the wait.

Reserve 1 cup of the coconut flakes. Mix the remaining 3 cups coconut flakes with the sour cream, sugar, and salt in a large bowl until smooth. Cover with plastic wrap and refrigerate until the coconut softens and the cream mixture thickens, at least 2 hours and up to overnight.

Preheat the oven to 350°F.

Spread the remaining coconut on a half-sheet pan. Bake, stirring occasionally, until golden, about 5 minutes. Let cool completely and reserve in an airtight container for up to 3 days.

Transfer the cake to a large cutting board. Trim the edges, then cut the cake into thirds crosswise to form three 11 by 5-inch rectangles. Place one rectangle on a cake platter. Stir the coconut frosting and spread one-third of it onto the cake. Top with another cake rectangle and half of the remaining frosting, then stack with the final cake rectangle and the remaining frosting.

Cover with plastic wrap and refrigerate to set, at least 3 hours. When ready to serve, unwrap and sprinkle the reserved toasted coconut on top.

Make ahead: The assembled cake can be refrigerated for up to 3 days.

Coconut Cake

MAKES ONE 12 BY 17 BY 1-INCH CAKE

12 tablespoons (6 ounces) unsalted butter, cut into tablespoons and softened, plus more for the pan

2 cups all-purpose flour, plus more for the pan

3/4 cup buttermilk

1/4 cup heavy cream

2 teaspoons pure vanilla extract

1 cup sugar

3 1/2 teaspoons baking powder

1/2 teaspoon baking soda

1 teaspoon salt

1/4 cup coconut oil

5 large eggs, at room temperature

Baking cake batter in a half-sheet pan gives you a thin layer that can be used in tons of ways. I cut it in rectangles and layer it with coconut cream (see page 292). You can cut out rounds for perfectly even layers without the tricky business of splitting a cake. (And you end up with scraps to snack on!) You can cut little squares and top with a dollop of frosting for one-bite treats. I like the hint of coconut in this mix, but you can swap in vegetable oil for a plain yellow cake too.

Preheat the oven to 350°F. Butter a half-sheet pan, line the bottom with parchment paper, and butter the parchment. Lightly dust with flour and tap out any excess.

Combine the buttermilk, cream, and vanilla in a medium bowl. Combine the flour, sugar, baking powder, baking soda, and salt in the bowl of a stand mixer. Beat with the paddle attachment on low speed until well mixed. Add the oil and beat until evenly distributed. The mixture will look like coarse sand. With the machine running, add the butter 1 tablespoon at a time and beat until fully incorporated.

Add the eggs one at a time, beating well after each addition and scraping the bowl occasionally. While beating, add the buttermilk mixture in a slow, steady stream. Beat just until smooth. Pour the batter into the prepared pan and spread evenly.

Bake until a tester inserted in the center comes out clean, about 20 minutes. When you gently press a fingertip into the top, the cake should not indent.

Let cool in the pan on a wire rack for 5 minutes. Invert onto the rack, peel off and discard the parchment, and let cool completely.

Make ahead: The cake keeps at room temperature tightly wrapped for up to 3 days.

Strawberry Cake

Cake

- 3 tablespoons unsalted butter, softened, plus more for the pan
- 1 cup all-purpose flour, plus more for the pan
- ½ cup plus 2 tablespoons granulated sugar
- 1 teaspoon baking powder
- ¼ teaspoon salt
- ¼ cup heavy cream
- ½ teaspoon pure vanilla extract
- 1 tablespoon vegetable oil
- 1 large egg
- 1 large egg yolk
- 1 cup (½ ounce) dehydrated strawberries, broken into small pieces

Strawberry cake's a Southern celebration, often appearing on Juneteenth picnic tables. As an emancipation food, it commemorates ingenuity and resilience in bondage. Traditionally, it's plain cake layered with strawberry buttercream. I've always wanted more strawberry flavor, so I put it in the cake and topping here. Dehydrated strawberries, now sold everywhere as snacks, moisten and soften in a cream cake batter, delivering super berry sweetness. Fresh berries get to shine all by themselves, sitting pretty in a whipped cream cloud.

For the cake: Preheat the oven to 350°F. Butter a 9-inch round cake pan. Line the bottom with parchment paper and butter the parchment, then flour the pan, tapping away any excess.

Combine the flour, granulated sugar, baking powder, and salt in the bowl of an electric mixer. Combine the cream and vanilla in a medium bowl.

Beat the dry ingredients with the paddle attachment on low speed until well mixed. Add the oil and beat until evenly distributed. With the machine running, add the butter 1 tablespoon at a time and beat until fully incorporated. The mixture will look like coarse sand.

Add the egg, then the egg yolk, beating well after each addition and scraping the bowl occasionally. While beating, add the cream mixture in a slow, steady stream. Beat just until smooth. Fold in the dehydrated strawberries until evenly distributed. Pour into the prepared pan.

Bake until the top springs back a little when gently pressed, 25 to 27 minutes.

Continued

Topping

³/₄ cup heavy cream

³/₄ cup sour cream

¹/₄ cup confectioners' sugar

1¹/₂ pounds small
    strawberries, hulled

Let cool in the pan on a wire rack for 5 minutes. The sides should have come loose from the pan. If not, run a knife around the side of the pan. Center a piece of parchment over the cake and invert onto a cutting board or another rack. Peel off the bottom parchment and invert the cake back onto the rack, top side up. Remove the top parchment. Let cool completely.

For the topping: Whisk the cream, sour cream, and confectioners' sugar until soft peaks form.

Transfer the cake to a serving plate. Dollop the cream over the cake, then top with the strawberries. Serve immediately.

Make ahead: The cake keeps at room temperature tightly wrapped for up to 3 days.

Drinks

Mango Coconut Frappé

2 mangoes, preferably champagne, peeled, pitted, and chopped

1 (15-ounce) can coconut milk, well shaken

2 tablespoons honey

2 teaspoons fresh lime juice

¼ teaspoon kosher salt

2 cups ice, plus more for serving

Lime seltzer, for serving

I call this my adult frappé. Nope, it doesn't have booze. But it's got everything else you want in a drink: a little sweetness and creaminess topped off with fizzy bubbles. Even though it isn't sugary, it has layers of flavors with tropical mango and coconut brightened by lime.

Puree the mangoes with the coconut milk, honey, lime juice, salt, and ice in a blender until smooth and frothy. Divide among 8 glasses filled with ice. Top off with lime seltzer.

Sweet Tea Soda

1 lemon, plus wedges for serving

2 cups sugar

6 black tea bags, paper tags cut off

3 liters unflavored, unsweetened soda water or seltzer

Mint sprigs, for garnish

A tall ice-filled glass of sweet tea is like a period on a sentence. It completes me. Add bubbles and *whoo whee*! Nothing's more refreshing. I model my mix on Granny's, Lipton tea bags and all. It's dark amber with a good pucker and not too sugary. To fizz up sweet tea, I make a lemony simple syrup and top it off with soda water right before serving. Of course, you can finish it with flat water too. If it's cocktail time, go ahead and stir in a shot of bourbon. Granny sure would've.

Remove the zest from the lemon in long strips with a vegetable peeler. Squeeze 1/4 cup juice from the lemon.

Combine the sugar and 2 cups water in a small saucepan and bring to a boil, stirring to dissolve the sugar. Add the tea bags and lemon zest and juice. Boil for 2 minutes. Remove from the heat and let steep for 40 minutes.

Discard the tea bags. Divide the syrup and zest among jars. Seal and chill until cold.

When ready to serve, fill tall glasses with ice. Pour 1/4 cup syrup into each glass, then top off with a generous cup of soda water. Garnish with mint and a lemon wedge and serve with a straw or swizzle stick for stirring.

Make ahead: The syrup can be refrigerated for up to 2 weeks.

Habanero Ginger Simple Syrup

MAKES 2½ CUPS

2 cups sugar

1 habanero chile, slit

2 slices fresh ginger

3 chai tea bags, tags cut off
    (optional)

This spiced and spicy syrup will become your cocktail and mocktail staple. Simply top it off with sparkling water. For a boozy brown drink, add a shot of bourbon. For a summer sparkler, try vodka.

Combine the sugar and 2 cups water in a medium saucepan and bring to a boil, stirring to dissolve the sugar. Add the chile, ginger, and tea bags, if using. Boil for 1 minute, then remove from the heat.

Let steep for 30 minutes. Discard the tea bags, if needed. Let the syrup cool to room temperature.

Make ahead: The syrup can be refrigerated for up to 2 weeks.

RED EMANCIPATION FOODS

There's a reason we raise a glass of red soda each Juneteenth. It's freedom. Juneteenth, which falls on the nineteenth of the month, commemorates the day Union soldiers freed slaves in Galveston, Texas. Two and a half years after the Emancipation Proclamation. Two and a half years, people. So, yes, the last slaves to be freed wanted to finally have what they couldn't. Big, big important things—their families, first and foremost. And small things that give us dignity daily, like choosing what we eat and drink.

Slaves were barred from having red soda, a nineteenth-century novelty. On June 19, 1865, the free popped open bottles and tasted sweet freedom.

Red food and drinks grace Juneteenth tables every year. For my take on emancipation foods, I turn to all the beautiful red ingredients nature gives us. Beets, red cabbage, red onions, peppers, and tomatoes for savory dishes. Berries for dessert. And watermelon for homemade red soda. Here's to freedom!

Watermelon Juice

Puree seeded watermelon until very smooth. If you want it a touch sweeter, blend in some simple syrup (page 302). Chill until very cold, then stir again before pouring over ice. If you want to turn the juice into a soda, top it off with seltzer water.

Cantaloupe Juice

Puree cantaloupe until very smooth. Serve immediately over ice or blend again before serving because the solids and fruit will separate.

Celebration Menus

CELEBRATION MENUS

Acknowledgments

FROM CARLA AND GENEVIEVE

We are so grateful to everyone who made this book possible. First and foremost, to the generations of cooks from Africa to America, from the past to the present, who have carried and carry on this rich culinary tradition. And to those who have documented it over the years, in official and unofficial capacities.

Much of our inspiration came from the road trip we took through the South to research this book. We are so grateful for the warmth and hospitality of everyone we met and especially to those who hosted us and shared their food and stories: 563 King for hosting us in Charleston; "The Pickle Lady" Rachelle E. Bennett at the Charleston farmers' market for her pickles, relish, and stories; chef Rodney Scott, general manager Chris Reeder, pit master Anya Hall, and the staff at Rodney Scott's Barbecue in Charleston for the good food and the tour of the pits; chef Charlotte Jenkins and Rita Jenkins for their Awendaw Gullah family food memories; chef Marvin Hall for sharing his food, stories, and fresh haul from South Carolina farmers; everyone at Mother Emmanuel African Methodist Episcopal Church in Charleston for welcoming us, and especially Sherry Stokes, the head of the culinary committee, for letting us into her kitchen; chef B.J. Dennis and his family for welcoming us into their home, feeding us, and telling us about their family, food, and reviving old ingredients; Ali Lentini and Andrew Chasson of CAA Culinary for coordinating our lodging through Staybridge and Candlewood Suites; chef and farmer Matthew Raiford and Jovan Sage for teaching us about the land, its history, and its ability to heal; Johno Morisano, chef Mashama Bailey, and the staff at the Grey in Savannah for a warming, welcoming meal; chef Joseph G. Randall for a tour of his favorite Savannah eats and his African American Chefs Hall of Fame; baker Cheryl Day for her cheer and good company; Lula Hatcher and Deborah Hatcher of Lannie's BBQ in Selma for that pork cracklin', inviting us in, and sharing intimate stories of the Civil Rights movement; Felicia A. Bell, director of the Rosa Parks Museum in Montgomery, for the personal tour of the exhibits; the crew of teenage tour guides at the Birmingham Civil Rights Institute made the museum come alive; chef Roscoe Hall for feeding us delicious food and great stories; chef John Hall for guiding us through Jones Valley Farm in Birmingham and telling us about his journey; Enrika Williams for her food tour of Jackson and for her embracing spirit; Glenda Barner and Marcus Dillard of Sugar's Place in Jackson for a warm welcome and soul food we'll never forget; to all the staff at Bully's in Jackson for hosting us with such enthusiasm; Cindy Ayers Elliot, Bill Evans, and Danny Murray of Footprint Farms in Jackson for bringing us to the land and letting us take from it; Beth Williams and all her staff for hosting us at the beautiful Alluvian Hotel in Greenwood,

Mississippi, and feeding us at Giardina; Andre Prince Jeffries and all the staff at Prince's Hot Chicken in Nashville for the best hot chicken in the world; Irene Long, the cake lady of Prince's, for her caramel cake and baking tales David Swett and all the staff at Swett's in Nashville for pushing those tables together for the Hall clan to gather and eat the meal they all love most; George Hall, Audrey Hall, Jacqueline Hall Majors, Kim Macedo, Daniel Hall, Charlie PettyJohn, Ariel Hall, and Charlette Hall for the best family reunion.

Huge thanks to our photo team, starting with our photographer, Gabriele Stabile, who captured food, people, and places with brilliance and heart. We're grateful for his flexibility in extending our road trip to shoot beauties impromptu, which wouldn't have been possible without the generosity of Jesse Goldstein of Food Sheriff Kitchen and Beth Robinson of KitchenAid. Thank you for providing the space and props in Nashville. Back in New York, we're grateful to Maya Rossi for choosing, mixing, and matching props with her tasteful eye; Corey Belle for shopping, prepping, and styling the dishes and keeping the shoot flowing; Jonathan Santiago for assisting; Zabela Moore for keeping the place tidy. Thank you to Jen Boroff and GE Appliances for providing an induction cooktop for the shoot.

We're thankful to those who made this book possible: Janis Donnaud lit a fire under us as agent; Karen Rinaldi championed our vision as editor; and the whole HarperWave team worked incredibly hard to make this book what it is and to get it into the world. Thanks to the editorial team of Hannah Robinson and Rebecca Raskin; designer Leah Carlson-Stanisic and cover designer Joanne O'Neill; Penny Makras in marketing and Yelena Nesbit in publicity. Kirsten Bischoff coordinated, scheduled, and kept everything and everyone on track.

We learned so much about the rich history of soul food through this book and are especially grateful to Tonya Hopkins for her research. The works of Edna Lewis, Jessica Harris, Michael Twitty, Toni Tipton-Martin, Leni Sorenson, and many others were invaluable as well. We're honored to be among the community of soul food cookbook authors and owe a debt of gratitude to everyone who has passed down recipes, stories, and knowledge and to those who continue to do so now.

FROM CARLA

To Gina Paige, founder of African Ancestry, and to Tonya Hopkins, food historian, for helping me discover those ancestors and learn more about my past, my people, our history.

To those who work tirelessly to help others and give me the opportunity to give back, especially Helen Keller International, for your work in Asia and Africa with sustainable farming and the empowerment of women, and CARE, for giving me the chance to work with you in Mozambique.

To Aunt Lucille, for the long conversations about food, our family, and her days as a caterer.

For the many hours of family storytelling with Mama, Daddy, Kim, Daniel, Bonita, Jackie, Nyemale, Basimah, and Kenneth.

For Mama, for giving me more food memories than I realized and for giving us the family time that created those memories.

For Genevieve Ko, my coauthor, for understanding why I needed to do this cookbook, and for helping me breathe life into it. Because of you, I continue to discover parts of myself.

To Gabriele Stabile, my photographer. Thank you for your perspective, for really seeing what's in front of you, and for capturing its truth.

For the ten-day southern road trip with Genevieve and Gabriele. The discoveries and rediscoveries of African-American culture, soul food, pride, and friendship that only a road trip can cultivate.

To Matthew, whose love and support are always my North Star. You make it possible for me to have one adventure after another.

FROM GENEVIEVE

I am so grateful to Carla for bringing me on this cookbook journey and for her friendship. For nearly a decade, you have been an inspiration, showing me the joy of being authentic and embracing heritage in the kitchen and outside of it.

This book wouldn't be what it is without Gabriele's photography. Thank you for capturing grace in every situation we put you in, no matter how challenging.

Thank you to Karen and the Harper Wave team for embracing our vision and giving us the freedom to run with it. To everyone who collaborated on this book, your teamwork made this project come together seamlessly. To all the people who so openly shared their stories and lives, thank you for letting me in.

My family rallied behind this project and welcomed it into our home. Thank you for your patience, support, and love.

Index

About the Authors

Carla Hall is a chef, television personality, lifestyle expert, and food activist. She was a cohost of the daytime food talk show *The Chew*, a finalist on the cooking competitions *Top Chef* and *Top Chef: All-Stars*, and regularly appears on the Food Network. Her path to culinary celebrity started after she graduated from Howard University and discovered her passion for cooking. She attended culinary school and went on to become executive chef in fine-dining restaurants and founded acclaimed businesses in catering and food retail. Carla is also the author of *Carla's Comfort Foods: Favorite Dishes from Around the World* and *Cooking with Love: Comfort Food That Hugs You*. In all these ventures and through her travels, Carla connects people through food and across cultures. In addition to her work with social justice, advocacy, and philanthropic organizations, Carla is the culinary ambassador for Sweet Home Café at the Smithsonian National Museum for African American History and Culture in Washington, DC, where she lives with her husband.

Genevieve Ko is the author of *Better Baking* and has collaborated on dozens of other cookbooks. She is the contributing food editor at *Shape* magazine and writes stories and develops recipes for other media outlets. Her work has been featured in the *New York Times* and the *Washington Post* as well. Genevieve lives in New York City with her family.